John Madin

Twentieth Century Architects

THE
TWENTIETH
CENTURY
SOCIETY

ENGLISH HERITAGE

RIBA ⊞ **Publishing**

John Madin

Twentieth Century Architects

Alan Clawley

© Alan Clawley, 2011

Published by RIBA Publishing, 15 Bonhill Street, London EC2P 2EA

ISBN 978 1 85946 367 3

Stock Code 73087

British Library Cataloguing-in-Publication Data
A catalogue record for this book is available from the British Library.

Publisher: Steven Cross
Commissioning Editor: Lucy Harbor
Series Editors: Barnabas Calder, Elain Harwood and Alan Powers
Project Editor: Susan George
Copy Editor: Ian McDonald
Typeset by Carnegie Book Production
Printed and bound by The Charlesworth Group, Wakefield

RIBA Publishing is part of RIBA Enterprises Ltd.
www.ribaenterprises.com

Front cover photo: The *Birmingham Post and Mail* Tower

Back cover photo: John Madin aged 36 at his drawing board

Frontispiece photo: 123 Hagley Road, JMDG offices

Foreword

*I hope to see in the near future a greater and a more beautiful Birmingham,
and I also wish that I shall be one of those lucky men who will, with care and
sympathy, be able to graft our City into the finest in the World. If this war
has ever done anything for the British people, it has given the enlightened
ones of the generation the chance to create a better and healthier place
to live in. The German bombs have stricken down so many of our towns'
buildings that it will be a simple matter to widen our thoroughfares and
build new offices and shops.*

Extract from 'The Future of Birmingham', by John Madin aged 16
17 December 1940

John Madin's teenage vision for Birmingham was not realised for its city centre, despite
his subsequent strong advocacy for a three-dimensional master plan for the area within
the future inner ring road. Nonetheless, his own contribution to Birmingham's recovery
in the aftermath of the war was significant and positive, in particular, Madin was
responsible for the master plan for the redevelopment of the 1625 acre Calthorpe Estate
(1958) just to the west of the city centre and much of its subsequent implementation, and
buildings within the city, such as the Chamber of Commerce, the Central Library, BBC
Pebble Mill and the Warwickshire Masonic Temple.

Madin's work, however, extends far beyond the bounds of Birmingham, including
projects as diverse and far afield as the master plan for Telford new town, the Yorkshire
Post and Mail Building, the radio and television complex (in association with Marconi)
in Zagreb, and the Wardija Hill Top Village in Malta.

Madin embraced Modernism at the Birmingham School of Architecture on
returning from war service in 1947. He visited Stockholm in 1949. Functionalism had
been the dominant architectural style in Sweden since its capital's exhibition of 1930;
Stockholm was also at the forefront of town planning. These factors, combined with the
fact that the city was a huge contrast to his war-ravaged home town, inspired Madin
and helped to crystallise his vision for Birmingham, illustrated in his 1951 Christmas
card, which included two sketches: one of Birmingham as he saw it then, the other as he
thought it should be.

For Madin, buildings should have an appearance of 'simplicity and sincerity', the
design of a building evolving from a full understanding of the brief, particularly through
its planning. He gives high importance to a building's relationship with its natural
surroundings, the linking of indoors and outside, the use of moving water, honestly

opposite: Warwickshire Masonic Temple, Clarendon Road, 2010

expressing materials and careful detailing Madin designed modernist-style fittings
and furnishings, including carpets, curtains, furniture door handles and even cutlery
to complement his buildings, and also commissioned and integrated work by well-
known artists of the day. Madin worked within the constraints of the labour force of the
time. The lack of skilled bricklayers in the 1950s, for example, led him to use concrete
frames for non-domestic buildings, cladding them within marble, granite or mosaic
finished panels, which also provided a self-cleansing surface to accommodate the
severe pollution of the time. He embraced new technology with component companies,
particularly the glazing manufacturer Henry Hope, and was also innovative in the
ways he found to minimise the impact of the car. From a base in his parent's study in
1950, Madin's practice grew by the mid-sixties into one of the largest multi-disciplinary
practices in the country, with a broad-based workload divided between the public and
the private sector, and between specialised one-off buildings and town planning work.
Madin's energy, enthusiasm and the trust clients had in him were essential ingredients
to his success. He was able to look beyond the client's initial brief at the bigger picture,
and was skilled at getting landowners, users, tenants and investors to work together
creatively.

When I was a child, my father would explain his initial ideas for a project to
me and on visiting a building or just recalling it; he would explain why it had been
designed in a particular way. I have found latterly working with him on projects has
helped me to appreciate his work more. Over the past year, I have been collating the
extensive Madin Archive, and adding current photography. This has provided the
opportunity to reflect on the projects with him, especially while visiting buildings
together. This process has on occasion identified where a building has been unsym-
pathetically altered, extended or has proved more financially attractive to redevelop.
The abiding memory, however, is positive: buildings being enjoyed and appreciated
by their users and sitting well within their planned landscaped environment. This
is particularly true in the Calthorpe Estate where the benefit of development in a
planned context is evident. Today, John Madin is as passionate about architecture and
planning as he was those 70 years ago as a sixteen year old.

Christopher Madin BA (Hons) Dip Arch RIBA

Acknowledgements

The idea of publishing a monograph of John Madin was first mooted by Eva Ling and Catherine Croft of the Twentieth Century Society as a means of boosting the campaign to stop Madin's Central Library in Birmingham from being demolished. Alan Powers generously endorsed my credentials for writing the book when that task fell to me. Elain Harwood of English Heritage brought her enthusiasm and knowledge to bear on the text and James Davies took a set of exciting new photographs.

The subject of the monograph, John Madin, has been fully behind the project from the start and has worked tirelessly with his son Christopher, to organise the enormous archive in the table tennis room at his home near Southampton, to provide illustrations, to write down his recollections and to correct any factual errors. Barrie Hall and Frank Brophy also contributed historical illustrations and John Ericsson and Lewis Jones added to the author's knowledge of the Madin firm.

My own exhibition, 'Back to the Modern', was held in the Central Library in 2006 thanks to Brian Gambles and Jerry Box in particular. It stimulated new interest in Madin's work while Andy Foster's excellent and detailed Pevsner guide to Birmingham buildings, which includes a whole chapter on the Library, provided lots of material and made him the obvious candidate to become Chair of Friends of the Central Library in 2007. Members of the Friends group have given their support to the book in various ways, particularly Iqbal Basi and Joe Holyoak.

Matthew Thompson, Lucy Harbor, Susan George and Neil O'Regan of RIBA Publishing made sure the book became a reality while at home my wife Hazel shared with me the inevitable stresses and strains of authorship.

ALAN CLAWLEY
DECEMBER 2010

THE
TWENTIETH
CENTURY
SOCIETY

Without the Twentieth Century Society an entire chapter of Britain's recent history was to have been lost. It was alert when others slept. It is still crucial!

Simon Jenkins, writer, historian, journalist

Love it or hate it, the architecture of the twentieth century has shaped our world: bold, controversial, and often experimental buildings that range from the playful Deco of seaside villas to the Brutalist concrete of London's Hayward Gallery.

Arguably the most vibrant, dynamic and expressive period of architecture in history, the twentieth century generated a huge range of styles. You don't have to love them all to believe that the best of these exciting buildings deserve to be protected, just like the masterpieces of the Victorian era that many likewise once thought to be eyesores. Buildings that form the fabric of our everyday life — office blocks, schools, flats, telephone boxes, department stores — are often poorly understood.

The campaign to protect the best of architecture and design in Britain from 1914 onwards is at the heart of the Twentieth Century Society. Our staff propose buildings for listing, advise on restoration and help to find new uses for buildings threatened with demolition. Tragedies like the recent demolition of the Modernist House Greenside, however, show how important it is to add your voice to the campaign.

Join the Twentieth Century Society, and not only will you help to protect these modern treasures, you will also gain an unrivalled insight into the groundbreaking architecture and design that helped to shape the century.

www.c20society.org.uk

opposite: Central Library, Birmingham in the mid-1980s with the Chamberlain Memorial in the foreground

BIRMINGHAM CITIZENS
PERMANENT BUILDING SOCIET

1 Madin and his work

The work of Birmingham architect John Madin and his associates was concentrated in two exciting and busy post-war decades when the West Midlands was the confident and wealthy centre of Britain's motor manufacturing. As the narrator René Cutforth noted in the British Broadcasting Corporation film *Six Men*, a study of power and influence in the city of Birmingham made in 1965, Madin was 'phenomenally successful'.[1] His success was due both to the quality of his work and to his formidable social skills, which were needed to handle the wide range of clients – from trades unions to captains of industry – that came to him with their projects. The values that characterise his architecture and planning work are attention to detail, careful research, use of natural materials, a liking for decoration and art in buildings, and a feeling for the modulation of interior and exterior space. He was trained in the modernist style, but was too much of a craftsman to abandon all decoration in his buildings. Madin's desire to look both forward and back, and to use natural materials in his buildings, appears often in his early small-scale work and even in some of his major commissions. When he could, he used coloured marble inlays, textured surfaces and works of art to relieve the uncompromising modernist aesthetic of his designs.

Madin's work closely reflects the evolution of the Modern Movement between 1950 and 1975. Moreover, his major buildings are concentrated in a compact area of Birmingham where their changing styles can be studied relatively easily – from the delicate early curtain walling with contrasting bands of materials to the later, strongly modelled concrete panels with their windows inset, and service towers of dark engineering brick.

Those who characterise Madin as a commercial architect because of his many and prominent office buildings should look at the other aspects of his practice, less glamorous but of great social significance. His conservationist approach to the development plan for the Calthorpe Estate; his workmanlike planning of Dawley, Telford and Corby new towns; his public-service commissions; and his design and layout of housing schemes that are still lived in and popular today – all these testify to his commitment to human values.

Madin believed in making a thorough study of the needs of his client before reaching a solution, even if the result looked like nothing else around at the time. The only problem with this approach was that if later the owners' needs changed, the building was unable to adapt with them. However, Madin was acutely aware that the way in which, for example, a library was used would change in the future, so he designed the Birmingham Central Library with floors that were free of columns and structural walls in order to permit a

opposite: **Birmingham Permanent Building Society offices, Bennetts Hill, c.1954**

flexible layout. He also researched the use of computers in the USA and provided for their impact on libraries by incorporating ducting in all the main floors.

This book cannot cover in detail all of Madin's built work, planning schemes and other projects. Until the original handwritten register of his commissions was digitised in December 2009, the full scale of his output was not known to the public and no definitive list was easily accessible. Only the most significant and well-known work across a range of building types and planning projects can be included and illustrated here. The Calthorpe Estate is given prominence as the foundation of Madin's later work, and the Central Library is highlighted for its part in bringing Madin's designs to national and international attention.[2] Detailed architectural descriptions are confined to examples that typify genres of his work, and to his most complex and award-winning buildings. The tally of awards won by Madin's buildings includes six from the Civic Trust, three from the Royal Institute of British Architects, and two (for housing) from the Ministry of Housing and Local Government. This collection indicates the high regard in which Madin's work was held, in their different ways, by lay people, fellow architects and government.

Architecture and planning in Birmingham

Birmingham has traditionally been associated more with manufacturing industry than with good architecture and, according to the major history of the city by Anthony Sutcliffe and Roger Smith, struggled to produce a strong local school of able architects.[3] Although Birmingham Corporation was famous in the 19th century for its municipal enterprise, there was often resistance to civic planning from its laissez-faire faction. By the 20th century, Birmingham's tradition of elevating enterprise over art was enshrined in the city council's policy of interfering as little as possible with developers' architects. The architect Joe Holyoak says that 'in the city's drive to attract investment, developers could set the agenda for planning', and while he was writing about the 1980s, the principle holds good throughout the century.[4]

Against this unpromising background, John Madin and James Roberts, whose Rotunda has become one of Birmingham's best known and iconic buildings, came to dominate architecture in their home city. Between them, they pioneered modern architecture for Birmingham's business community when there was none in the city. All Britain's major regional UK cities were slow to adopt Modernism, and Birmingham-trained students such as Frederick Gibberd and F. R. S. Yorke made their names in London in the 1930s, since architectural taste in Birmingham was not as adventurous as that in the capital city. Birmingham's first Modern Movement building was Brearley Street Nursery School, built by W. T. Benslyn in 1938–9 when Madin was still a teenager.[5] Andy Foster, author of the Pevsner architectural guide to Birmingham, maintains that the city saw nothing else like it for 20 years. Tecton's work at Dudley Zoo, completed in 1938, was one of the few other examples of modern design to be seen in the West Midlands at the time.

Town planning and urban design in Birmingham have followed the rise and fall of the city's economic fortunes and the ebb and flow of its resident population. However, alongside commerce there grew another tradition, of energetic private and philanthropic enterprise. George Cadbury bought farmland on the edge of the city and employed his own architects to plan and build Bournville in 1905. After the Second World War, it was to be the Calthorpe Plan (see Chapter 2), commissioned by a privately owned estate, that moderated the impact of private development, rather than the actions of the city planners. In 1950, when Madin started his practice, architects approached town planning as a natural extension of the design of individual buildings. State-funded new towns, universities and housing schemes had to be planned, and before the mid-1950s architects were almost the only professionals capable of doing this. It was to them that government ministers turned in order to realise their ideas.

Most of Birmingham's pre-1919 housing survived the Second World War, but by 1950 the poorer properties within a mile of the city centre had been identified as unfit for human habitation. Part of the problem was overcrowding, and the provision of new homes with adequate kitchens and bathrooms invariably meant that fewer people could be accommodated than before, raising the question of what to do with the remainder, or 'overspill'. Birmingham was corseted by a green belt, and was forced to build the Chelmsley Wood Estate in neighbouring Solihull to satisfy its appetite for expansion. The city had to look further beyond its boundaries to build more. Rehousing Birmingham people at Dawley, in Shropshire, began under the Town Development Act of 1952, and the Midlands New Town Society's influential campaign for more new towns paved the way for Madin to be able to do at Telford what he most wanted to do – design a completely new environment for people from start to finish. In the 1960s, it seemed that anything was possible. Architects were given the task of building entire new communities. They believed that a new environment would make better people, people who appreciated what was being done for them, and it was difficult for them to avoid being to some extent socialist in outlook. Many architects worked in local authorities and government agencies, and leading architects in private practice were also reliant on commissions from the expanding public sector.

The economic downturn of the 1970s only accentuated the steady demise of the UK's public-sector housing programme. The government had already abolished most of its subsidies for building housing over six storeys high before the catastrophic collapse of Ronan Point in May 1968 marked the end of local authority tower-block building. Birmingham City Council built its last example in 1971. Without the planned towers the Calthorpe Park scheme that Madin designed for the city council remained incomplete and unbalanced, unlike his mixed-density schemes on the Calthorpe Estate, such as High Point, which retain their integrity today.

The West Midlands became a high-wage economy during the 1950s and 1960s, and this coincided with the growth of Madin's architectural practice. His earliest clients came from both sides of manufacturing industry as well as from commerce. Both employers and unions commissioned Madin's young modern practice to design brand

new headquarters buildings in the city, and the Chamber of Commerce appointed him to design its new head offices.

The durability of Madin's buildings was brought to the author's attention by an article in the *Birmingham Post* for 14 May 2002, in which the city council claimed that his Central Library was 'crumbling'. Any degree of scrutiny showed that this was clearly not the case, and a long campaign to give to one of his best and most important buildings the credit it was due and to save it from destruction led eventually to the writing of this book.

The text is based on frequent conversations and correspondence between John Madin and the author since 2006. The main source of documentary material is Madin's extensive collection of photographs, press cuttings and papers at his home outside Southampton. A collection of photographs has been compiled by members of the Birmingham Architectural Association, many of which have already been added to the Southampton archive. Birmingham Central Library provided archive photographs for the author's exhibition 'Back to the Modern' in 2006, but the 600 boxes of papers from Madin's office remain in storage pending the appointment of an archivist. Frank Brophy also looks after a sizeable collection of photographs and architectural drawings at the Hockley office of Brophy Riaz Architects. There is, therefore, still much original material to catalogue and for architects and architectural historians to study.

above: John Madin aged 36 at his drawing board

Three short presentations to
celebrate the work of one of
Birmingham's most important
architects, **John Madin**.

MADIN
BIRMINGHAM

14 September 2007, 6pm | Library Theatre | Central Library | Birmingham

Early years and formative influences

John Hardcastle Dalton Madin was born in Moseley, Birmingham, on 23 March 1924
and was an only child. His father William was a master builder and cabinetmaker, who
taught the young John bricklaying and carpentry, while his mother Hilda was very
artistic and encouraged her son to draw and paint. The Madins lived in a detached
Victorian villa at No.158 Yardley Wood Road, Moseley, where father and son built
a conservatory and an extension together. Madin went to Stanley House School in
Edgbaston, and by the age of 12 was convinced that he had to be an architect. During
the Second World War the family spent some time on their Warwickshire smallholding,
where Madin used to shoot rabbits and sell them in Birmingham for pocket money.

On leaving school in 1940 at the age of 16, Madin found a job in the Corporation
Architect's offices at the Council House in Birmingham city centre. One of his duties
was taking the City Engineer, Herbert Manzoni (1899–1972), his lunch while he sat
next to the large coal fire in his office. When Birmingham was bombed in 1940,
Madin undertook fire-watch duty from the clock tower of the Council House, from
which he could see most of the city centre and mark on a map where the bombs had
fallen. This may have helped him develop an awareness of town planning that would
be useful later.

above: 'Madin Birmingham', flier for event at Artsfest 2007

Encouraged by Manzoni, Madin began his studies in the autumn of 1940 at the
Birmingham School of Architecture, then part of the School of Art in Margaret Street,
close to the Council House. The architecture school had been founded in 1909 and still
maintained Birmingham's Arts and Crafts tradition, a legacy that found its way into
Madin's early work.[6] In 1942, towards the end of the second year of his course and at
the age of 18, Madin decided with two fellow students to volunteer for the RAF in order
to (in his words) 'shoot down the German bombers'. After six months' training he was
told he could not be a pilot because of a defect in his night vision, so he joined the Royal
Engineers and was first a lieutenant in India and Iraq, and then a staff captain in Egypt.
There he supervised German prisoners of war building accommodation for service
families by the Suez Canal until 1947.

Madin returned to Birmingham to find the centre of the city 'in a terrible state,
bombed out buildings, [with] sites in New Street and Corporation Street used for
second-hand car sales'.[7] He completed his course at the School of Architecture with the

above left: Madin's 1951 Christmas card, Birmingham then
above right: Madin's Christmas Card 1951, Birmingham as it should be

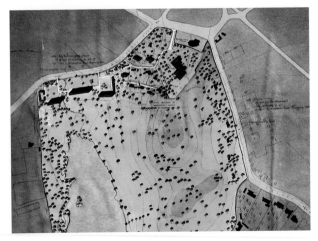

experience of war and foreign travel, and the sight of his depressed and damaged home city compelled him to create a better world. This was not only the optimism of youth and the enthusiasm of making a new start. From the Modern Movement, by now well established elsewhere if not in Birmingham, he acquired an aesthetic language that also spoke of a clean break with the past. His architectural training gave him the tools for the job. Madin's 4th year thesis was a housing project on the site of Edgbaston Golf Course. He proposed a line of elegant blocks that carefully preserved the landscape which he felt so valuable and presaging his later work, particularly that in Edgbaston.

Many years later, in an interview with Anthony Sutcliffe, Madin rated the Birmingham School of Architecture 'one of the big three', the others being Liverpool and the Architectural Association (AA) in London. Asked whether the school was connected with a particular style or approach to architecture, like a smaller version of the Bauhaus, Madin did not think that it typecast its students in that way, but did remember in 1948 a senior lecturer suddenly telling the students that training

above: **Perspective and site plan of Madin's student project**

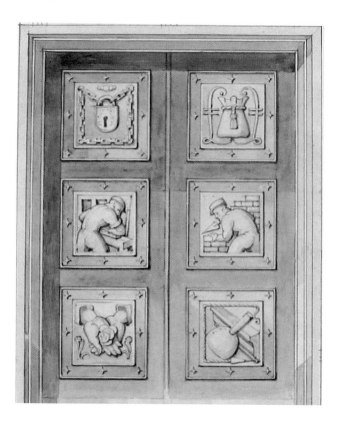

in classical architecture was being abandoned. Madin was clearly impressed by this change, which he recalls happened at Liverpool and the AA at the same time.[8] While still a student, Madin was invited to design alterations to the city-centre premises for the Birmingham Citizens Building Society, opened in 1951 in Colmore Row.

In 1949, his final year of studies, Madin hitch-hiked around Scandinavia with a fellow student and was extremely impressed with the Swedish version of Modernism, particularly the buildings he saw in Stockholm. He later visited the United States, when he was given a letter of introduction to Frank Lloyd Wright. In New York, Madin met Walter Gropius and recorded a conversation with him.

First practice – John H. D. Madin, 1950–1962

After a 12-week spell with architects J. B. Surman and Partners following his graduation, Madin was admitted as an associate member of the RIBA and started his own practice from his parents' home in Moseley, designing new houses and repairing those damaged by war. A year or two later he invited two of his contemporaries at the

above: Madin's design for the front doors of the Birmingham Citizens Permanent Building Society

Birmingham School of Architecture, Tom Hood and Doug Smith, to join him. His
first office was in a couple of Victorian houses at Nos.83–5 Hagley Road, leased from
the Calthorpe Estate and renovated with the help of his father. The shop-front for the
Citizens Permanent Building Society at No.16 Bennetts Hill was noticed by the City
Architect, A. G. Sheppard Fidler, who was sufficiently impressed to invite Madin in 1954
to design a local shopping centre on the new council estate at Woodcock Hill, which
was opened in 1957. This job led to similar work on new council estates at Jiggins Lane,
Deelands Road, Rubery and in Kingshurst.

above top: **Local shopping centre for the City Council**
above: **House for Mr Tranter, Kidderminster**

above top: The Engineering Employers Federation Headquarters, 1957
above: The Engineering Employers Federation Headquarters, 2010

In this phase of his practice, Madin designed over 40 houses for private individuals either on the Calthorpe Estate, such as St Georges Close and Westbourne Gardens, or on individual sites elsewhere in Birmingham and the West Midlands. Some, like Oldnall Road, Kidderminster, have fallen victim to rising land values and have been demolished to make way for more intensive development. The best of them are included in the list of works at the end of this book.

Madin became a committee member of the Birmingham and Five Counties Architectural Association in 1955. (The counties in question were Herefordshire, Worcestershire, Warwickshire, Staffordshire and Shropshire.) The next year, he married Judith Jackson. Interviewed years later, Madin revealed how he had met her. He had 'once taken a complete day off; about ten years ago. He'd gone to the local tennis club at Edgbaston. That's how he met Judith, a hospital almoner. Her hobby was evening classes in architecture.'[9] Their first married home was at No.1 Lyttleton Road, Edgbaston, which Madin had converted in 1956 into three flats to his own designs. From 1960 to 1975, they lived with their son and two daughters in a house designed by Madin in St Georges Close, Edgbaston.

Asked by Sutcliffe in 1969 how he came by his work, Madin replied:

> The commissions which we get are purely fortuitous. I have no idea why the Calthorpe Estate approached me, unless it was because I had just completed a small office block for the Engineering and Allied Employers' Federation. But these commissions naturally led me on to getting a commission to design the new Chamber of Commerce, at the official opening of which I was asked [by the Chairman of the newspaper group himself] to do the new building for the Birmingham Post and Mail.[10]

The Engineering Employers' Federation building was commissioned in 1954, and was Madin's first major building. In 1960 it was among the first buildings to be given a Civic Trust Award, a scheme initiated in 1959; Madin was to win six of these awards in the course of his career.

The accommodation included a boardroom; a suite for trades union officials; and offices for the chairman, director, secretary and other administrative staff. They were carefully designed with pleasant proportions and excellent materials, in order to facilitate civilised relations between the two sides of industry. The principal rooms are on the first floor, which is clad in travertine, over a ground floor that is slightly set back – perhaps an acknowledgement of Le Corbusier's Villa Savoye. At the corner is a recessed entrance that was to become a Madin characteristic, behind a fluted pier cut back at the top and a freestanding slate slab cut with diamond patterns. Madin designed the carpets, door furniture, curtains and panelling, all of which have been maintained by the owners.

In the film *Six Men*, Madin describes how he designed the building to harmonise with the adjacent Georgian terrace, by the use of plain white surfaces, well-proportioned windows and matching storey heights. He felt that it was important

that the building should 'sell' modern architecture to the business community. Although narrator Cutforth astutely comments that it did not break new ground as a piece of architecture, it was and remains a most careful and competent design – one which convinced Birmingham businessmen that its architect could be trusted to design modern buildings of quality that were not too outlandish for their conservative taste. As Cutforth commented:

> *Madin keeps a strong sense of the demands of the client. Personal vision is kept on the curb but it's there alright ... An architect may seethe with exciting ideas but in the end he stands and falls by what he has done. He is not allowed to advertise – he hopes his buildings will do that for him. Madin's advertisements are all over Birmingham today. Birmingham's taste in architecture has never been very highly regarded. The city's tycoons must be reassured nowadays to have an OK architect among them.*[11]

Although the Engineering Employers' building was a modern functional structure, Madin included a purely decorative screen wall to moderate its severity. The elegant overhanging roof also softens its purity of form. The balcony floor slabs are as thin as possible, and give a lightness to the design. The building is still in use today, in excellent condition with few alterations, and its owners are to be commended for their stewardship.

above left: The Engineering Employers Federation Headquarters, entrance
above right: The Engineering Employers Federation Headquarters, entrance screen detail

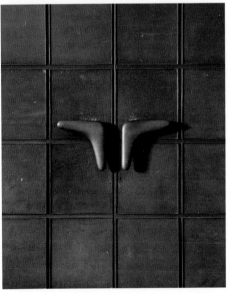

above top: The Engineering Employers Federation Headquarters, view into boardroom from reception
above left: The Engineering Employers Federation Headquarters, boardroom doors detail
above right: The Engineering Employers Federation Headquarters, entrance door handles

Expansion – John H. D. Madin & Partners, 1962–1967

Twelve years after its foundation, the practice had grown so much that it was necessary to take on three architect partners, and in 1963 they moved to Radclyffe House in Edgbaston. Madin's original colleagues and Cliff Downing were given a small share in the practice.

By 1965, when Madin was filmed by the BBC, his practice occupied new purpose-built offices at No.123 Hagley Road, housing over 150 staff. Cutforth observed that:

> The men and women who work here are enthusiastic, eager and highly profes-sional. The firm's reputation ensures a steady stream of applicants to join it, though an equally large number would no doubt rather work in an architect's department in one of the big cities with its more obvious social application. Housing for people or a Masonic temple? Perhaps not a fair contrast, but to many people in the profession this is the sort of contrast that springs to their minds in connection with the Madin firm.[12]

Madin strongly believed that profit, although necessary, should not be the only value determining the outcome of his work. He tried his utmost to get the best for the client whether it was a private business or a new town corporation. Reflecting in *Six Men* on a visit to the USA, he said that:

> America today in many ways is most disappointing. The greater wealth and physical development have not borne a finer way of life. They have produced conditions which are nauseating in many respects. Values are twisted towards the most important factor – the almighty dollar. All other values in the end seem to be subservient to this great motivating force. America is a country of the individual, a country where the freedom of the individual is so important that recognition is only just being given to the fact that freedom for all in a closely knit society without concern for the community as a whole must ultimately end in the destruction of the very social and economic environment which is so desperately sought after by so many. This is shown by the confusion and the problems of the administrative machinery and the almost impossible conditions which make it extremely difficult to implement any planned proposals, either socially or economically. And certainly, physical planning in terms of urban renewal is almost impossible at the present time. The lack of planning has caused considerable wastage and here in Britain we just cannot afford to waste our resources by having to pull down buildings and reconstruct roads due to the inadequacy of planning for the future, as they have in America today.[13]

The film also explored Madin's role in the firm, said to be the third-largest private practice in the country at the time. Cutforth asks, 'And what is the role of the boss in this sort of organisation? Is he a stimulator of effort and ideas or an artist? Or is he an organisation man, a good brisk salesman? Or is he in fact a bit of both, artist and salesman, walking a rather precarious tightrope between inspiration and diplomacy?' As founder and principal of the practice that bore his name, Madin was of course

legally and professionally responsible for every drawing that left the office. Over images of a board meeting, he commented that:

> I have nine partners, all of whom play a vital role in the development of any building or planning project ... Some architects and planners put themselves over as the great creator but this isn't really so. They rely very largely on their team. Many buildings are spoilt by architects designing a building their client can't afford and then having to cut back, so that underneath the desire to create fine buildings one must have a basic idea as to whether the client can afford it and whether he can ultimately pay for it.[14]

John Madin Design Group, 1967–1989

Madin formed the John Madin Design Group in 1967, and was its senior partner until 1975. During this time, the practice was large enough to occupy three floors of No.123 Hagley Road. Madin initially gave three of his staff a small share in the practice, while

above: The BBC film crew on the terrace of Madin's house, 1965

making seven other employees salaried partners and promoting two more to associate partners. The practice employed its own quantity surveyors, an office manager and a librarian. Ian Standing, who started work in 1980 for the firm, recalls that Madin's ambition was to establish a hotbed of like-minded professionals working both inside and outside the practice; among others, Ove Arup & Partners came to Birmingham and joined him as engineers for the Central Library.[15]

The practice was divided into three functional sections – Design, Detail and Supervision. Madin personally brought the work into the office and was always head of Design. He insists that he initiated every project by sketching out his design concepts. Perhaps inspired by Le Corbusier's 'Modulor', Madin used the Golden Section in proportioning his buildings. Even after the initial ideas were passed over to the Detail section for working drawings to be produced, Madin kept a close eye on their development. The staff who then supervised the contractors on site were carefully chosen for their technical and managerial skills, yet Madin acted as the overall quality controller.

The huge workload and the complexity of the designs produced by the firm at its peak depended on many colleagues from a wide variety of disciplines. Madin was very good at assembling teams of people to run complex projects. As in most organisations some left to start their own practice, while others stayed for many years. The work on planning Telford demanded a large multi-disciplinary team for a number of years, at the end of which some members moved on to academic posts in disciplines other than architecture. Ian Standing reflected in 2005 that 'as with the best firms at any point in time, Madin's spawned lots of other practices: Cliff Downing, Tom Hood and Douglas Smith all left to set up their own. Derek Davies, Michael Haywood and Michael Holt were partners prior to 1975, and others, including Douglas Hickman and Fred Mark, deserve mention as important contributors to the practice's work.'[16] Madin remembers Hood, Smith and Downing saying that the practice had become too large for their liking. He generously gave them some of the projects on which they were working in order to start their independent careers.

The *Six Men* film reminds us with a shock how 'low-tech' an architect's office was in 1965. Models and drawings on the wall were the primary means of visual communication. Drawing boards with parallel motions, T-squares, variable-angle set squares and slide rules were the tools of the architect's trade. Special presentations were hand drawn and tinted with watercolour, gouache, crayon, pencil or coloured adhesive films. Lettering was applied by pressure on plastic sheets of letters on to cartridge paper or tracing paper. Madin made extensive use of block models and detailed architectural models to explain his designs to his clients. They were mostly made in the office by a former carpenter whom Madin brought into the practice. Writing in 2009, after the impact of computers on the architectural profession had been absorbed, Juhani Pallasmaa expressed his reservations about their use: 'The computer creates a distance between the maker and the object, whereas drawing by hand or building a model puts

the designer in skin-contact with the object or space.'[17] The hardware and software that made computer-aided design practicable were not available until the early 1980s but, according to the 1968 *John Madin Design Group Blue Book*, the practice was one of the first in the UK to introduce computer controls for project costings.

Work by artists was often incorporated into buildings designed by the Arts and Crafts architects, and, absorbing the links between this movement and Modernism, Madin continued this tradition whenever the opportunity arose. He persuaded the Birmingham Chamber of Commerce to allow John Piper to make a mural inside its new building, and elsewhere in the city he employed sculptor William Mitchell to design a series of concrete sculptural panels on Rail House and a set of decorative doors for the NatWest Centre.

The John Madin Design Group International, 1970–1989

In 1970, Madin formed a second practice with an office in Lausanne, Switzerland. He had been getting overseas commissions since 1966, and found it increasingly difficult to obtain exchange-control permission to carry out work abroad from the UK. The problem came to a head in 1970 with a major commission from Yugoslavian television. From then on, the international practice was expanded, with UK staff moving to

above: **The staff of JMDG with Madin outside 123 Hagley Road, 1975**

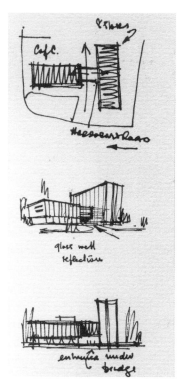 

Switzerland to work on commissions for other television centres and a string of leisure projects in France, Spain, Malta, Cyprus, Libya and the USA.

In 1974, Madin returned from an exhausting trip abroad feeling unwell and a minor heart condition was diagnosed. He decided to retire as the senior partner and to hand over the day-to-day running of the John Madin Design Group to his partners and associates. It was agreed in 1975 that Madin should continue to act as a consultant to the practice, subsequently known as 'JMDG', while retaining sole responsibility for the John Madin Design Group International and for earlier commissions. Some of the holiday-village projects that Madin had designed on the Mediterranean islands were, however, frustrated by local regime changes and, in the case of Cyprus, the Turkish invasion of 1974. After 1976, Madin's overseas workload was confined to projects in the Middle East, Mallorca and the USA. JMDG continued to operate in the UK until 1989, when it was formally wound up.

Madin continues to practise under his own name, and in 2010 is still heavily involved with a holiday village at Aberdyfi. He takes a close interest in saving the Birmingham Central Library from demolition.

above left: **Sketches for the Chamber of Commerce building**
above right: **Engineering Employers Federation**

Notes

1. René Cutforth narrating the BBC2 documentary series *Six Men*, broadcast in 1965.

2. Lucinda Lambton, in *Listed*, on BBC Radio Four (10 October 2008), interviewed the City Librarian inside the Central Library and the author on the steps outside. The other buildings in Lambton's programme, as listed in the *Radio Times*, 4–10 October 2008, under the title 'Defend Or Demolish?', were Robin Hood Gardens by Alison and Peter Smithson and the Plymouth Civic Centre by Jellicoe, Ballantine and Coleridge.

3. Anthony Sutcliffe and Roger Smith, *Birmingham 1939–1970*, 1974, pp460–1.

4. Joe Holyoak quoted in Ian Latham and Mark Swenarton, eds., *Brindleyplace*, 1999, p19.

5. Andy Foster, *Pevsner Architectural Guides: Birmingham*, 2005, writes on p178: 'The wings look like 1965, with cantilevered concrete balconies and flying staircases.'

6. ibid., pp20–6, argues that the Arts and Crafts movement 'stresses honest construction and values straightforward building methods'. This resonates strongly with Madin's approach and with the tenets of the future Brutalist movement. W. H. Bidlake taught at the School of Art from 1893, and W. R.

Lethaby lectured twice there in 1901, the second talk being his account of Morris as a work-master.

7. From text of speech made by John Madin to the West Midlands Royal Institute of British Architects (RIBA) on the occasion of the presentation of his Service to Industry Award, November 2005.

8. Interview by Anthony Sutcliffe, bound typescript held at Birmingham Central Library (LF71). In fact, the change happened slightly earlier at the AA and Liverpool.

9. Interview by Olga Franklin, 'This is the house Britain's busiest architect built for himself …', *Daily Mail*, 30 December 1964.

10. Sutcliffe, *op. cit.*

11. Cutforth narrating in Cutforth, *op. cit.*

12. ibid.

13. Madin speaking in Cutforth, *op. cit.*

14. ibid.

15. Ian Standing, in the (unpublished) text of his speech at the RIBA in 'John Madin: RIBA West Midlands Service To Industry Award' (Citation address), 2007.

16. ibid.

17. Juhani Pallasmaa, *The Thinking Hand: Existential and Embodied Wisdom in Architecture*, 2009, p97.

2   The Calthorpe Plan

The Calthorpe Estate lies in Edgbaston, a mile to the west of Birmingham's city centre and with the busy Hagley Road defining its northern boundary. The estate was formed by the Gough-Calthorpe family in the 18th century, and by the start of the First World War its 650 hectares (1,600 acres) had been thinly developed with large Victorian mansions for big families with servants, each house surrounded by extensive mature gardens. By the 1950s, under the stewardship of Brigadier Sir Richard Anstruther-Gough-Calthorpe (1908–1985), the second Baronet Calthorpe, some of the large properties along the Hagley Road had been converted to offices or had become run-down and even abandoned. Many leases were about to expire.[1]

The Master Plan

In 1957, five years after starting his practice in Edgbaston, Madin renovated an office for himself at Nos.83–5 Hagley Road, and completed his first major building on the Calthorpe Estate: the headquarters of the Engineering Employers Federation. Madin did not know that the Estate Manager had already seen and liked his work, at the time when Sir Richard Calthorpe was seeking advice on how to develop the estate. An introductory meeting with Sir Richard was arranged, during which Madin recommended that a master plan was needed. Sir Richard straight away invited him to draw it up.

The main conditions of the master plan were set on the one hand by the Calthorpe Estate and on the other by the city council in its 1952 Development Plan. The former wanted to retain the open character of the estate and raise more income from its property, the latter to increase the population density. Madin recommended that the required density of 75 persons per hectare (pph, or 30 persons per acre – ppa) could be achieved while maintaining the landscape quality of the estate, by mixing pockets of 250 pph (100 ppa) in high flats, 150 pph (60 ppa) in walk-up flats or terraced housing, and 37 pph (15 ppa) in individual houses. He also reserved 28 hectares (70 acres) of land between Hagley Road and Calthorpe Road for city-centre businesses displaced by wartime bombing. His proposal for a series of tall office blocks set back from the main road in their own landscaped setting seems commonplace today but in the Birmingham of 1957, where the City Engineer Manzoni set the façades of new buildings hard against his Inner Ring Road so as to generate maximum returns for the city, it was strikingly novel.

The uneasy relationship between Madin and Manzoni was later recalled by Anthony Sutcliffe from an interview with Madin. The latter argued that his Hagley Road offices were designed three-dimensionally in their own precincts, and provided perfectly

opposite: Calthorpe Estate Housing – Stonebury and Elmhurst, 2005

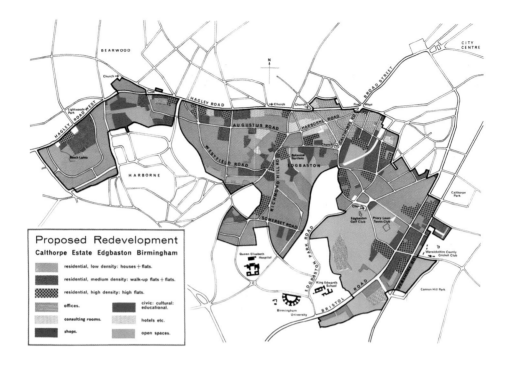

Proposed Redevelopment
Calthorpe Estate Edgbaston Birmingham

- residential, low density: houses + flats.
- residential, medium density: walk-up flats + flats.
- residential, high density: high flats.
- offices.
- consulting rooms.
- shops.
- civic: cultural: educational.
- hotels etc.
- open spaces.

acceptable returns to commercial developers. As Madin reflects, 'Manzoni was a road engineer. He was a fine person, and a great friend of mine, but this was his limitation.' In Edgbaston, Madin had the opportunity of applying his theory. He also insisted that only one third of each plot should be covered by buildings, leaving a third for car parking, and a third for landscaping. His master plan could have been seen as a rival to the traditional central business area, but to his surprise it was approved by the city council in 1958, and work began straight away to implement it.

Building the Plan

In setting out his design philosophy for the Calthorpe Estate, Madin wrote in 1958, 'It is hoped that the new buildings will be inspired with the spirit of the age and reflect in clear, modern lines, the beauties of the past and the strength and dignity of this era and the future. The best of the old is being carefully preserved, and it is believed, will be enhanced by the precise lines of the architecture of today.'[2] He quickly established a limited range of design motifs that he applied to his housing projects in a variety of ways. They are still easily discernible today – dark brown tile-hanging between windows, walls of natural brickwork, balconies and timber shiplap fascias. He used pitched roofs on individual bungalows and family houses, but flat roofs for terraces

above: The Calthorpe Estate master plan

above top: The cover of the 'Window on Edgbaston' brochure, 1962
above: Lord Calthorpe, Madin and developer with model of High Point

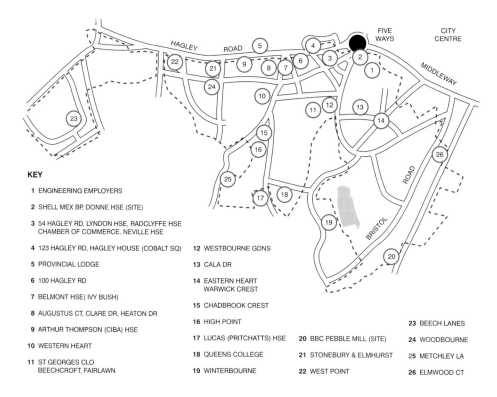

FIVE WAYS

CITY CENTRE

HAGLEY ROAD

MIDDLEWAY

ROAD

BRISTOL

KEY

1 ENGINEERING EMPLOYERS

2 SHELL MEX BP, DONNE HSE (SITE)

3 54 HAGLEY RD, LYNDON HSE, RADCLYFFE HSE
   CHAMBER OF COMMERCE. NEVILLE HSE

4 123 HAGLEY RD, HAGLEY HOUSE (COBALT SQ)

5 PROVINCIAL LODGE

6 100 HAGLEY RD

7 BELMONT HSE(IVY BUSH)

8 AUGUSTUS CT, CLARE DR, HEATON DR

9 ARTHUR THOMPSON (CIBA) HSE

10 WESTERN HEART

11 ST GEORGES CLO
    BEECHCROFT, FAIRLAWN

12 WESTBOURNE GDNS

13 CALA DR

14 EASTERN HEART
    WARWICK CREST

15 CHADBROOK CREST

16 HIGH POINT

17 LUCAS (PRITCHATTS) HSE

18 QUEENS COLLEGE

19 WINTERBOURNE

20 BBC PEBBLE MILL (SITE)

21 STONEBURY & ELMHURST

22 WEST POINT

23 BEECH LANES

24 WOODBOURNE

25 METCHLEY LA

26 ELMWOOD CT

and tower blocks. Madin's office was kept busy designing housing in Edgbaston from 1958 until 1973. Most of the housing schemes were produced for Artizans/Vista Developments, a subsidiary of the Calthorpe Estate, while some 20 private detached houses were designed for individual clients. By 1962, the Calthorpe Estate was confident that enough progress had been made on the development of the Estate to mount an exhibition entitled 'Window on Edgbaston'.

The brochure that accompanied the exhibition included a revised zoning plan and photographs of the completed buildings, as well as artist's impressions and illustrations of models and plans showing projects yet to come, including a residential tower block.[3] The publicity was designed to attract investors and future residents – and, most specifically, young housewives and their families – to Edgbaston. The prototype house was marketed as the 'Integro', and there was a choice of high-rise flats, medium-rise apartments, detached two-storey houses and single-storey patio houses.

Madin began the residential development of the Calthorpe Estate with private commissions from individual clients. The first was Heaton Drive, a new 'close' that was opened off Augustus Road. Madin designed a detached bungalow, No.10, with a pitched

above: **Map of Madin's work in the Calthorpe Estate**

roof and a gentle curve on plan that humanised its Modernism, an idea that appears
in later buildings, and No.12, a larger two-storey house with a pitched roof. These and
seven other houses in the close were all completed by 1959.

The first extended housing scheme was completed on Westbourne Road in 1959,
on the site of two large Victorian villas (one of them named Fairlawn) that had stood
in large gardens facing the road. Between 1959 and 1964, a total of 44 flats and eight
private houses were designed and built here. On the western half, which became St
Georges Close, Madin completed, in 1959, two three-storey terraces with 22 apartments
each – Beechcroft in St Georges Close and Fairlawn on the Westbourne Road – for the
Artizans group of companies. The Civic Trust gave Madin one of its coveted awards for
the two terraces.

The early humanist, nature-respecting schemes of the kind built at Beechcroft remain
popular. The mature trees, carefully retained in Madin's layout, gave the new housing a
head start, a point that the Civic Trust must have noticed. Natural features had similarly
been incorporated in the London County Council's estates at Roehampton, built in
1951–60, while Eric Lyons had made use of an existing market garden in his first Span
scheme at Parkleys, near Richmond in South London. Nikolaus Pevsner wrote that the

above: **Front elevation of Fairlawn**

synthesis of buildings and nature was bound to become an English task, and Madin's work in Egbaston exemplifies this.[4] There are also close affinities between Madin's work and Span housing in the use of weatherboarding and tile hanging within a modernist aesthetic, and in the use of covenants to control future development.

Madin then designed five detached houses on St Georges Close in 1960, including one for himself at No.20, and one for his friend Bill Scrase at No.18. Therefore, Madin not only lived on the estate for which he was the master planner but he occupied one of Birmingham's earliest examples of modernist architecture, designed by himself. In 1991, the Madin house became the subject of a conservation debate. The *Birmingham Post* described it as a classic example of the best of 1960s architecture, designed to allow the neighbours uninterrupted views over the green fields of Birmingham University campus. However, its new owner thought it was 'just a very ordinary post-war design'.[5] Madin's fear that the owner would ruin his design was dramatically realised when the house was demolished, despite having been in a Conservation Area since 1975.

In the eastern half of the site, which became known as Westbourne Gardens, Madin designed a two-storey terrace of four apartments, Nos.1–7 Westbourne Road, and three detached private houses. He later adapted one of these, No.12 Westbourne Gardens, for Alec Issigonis, the designer of the British Motor Corporation's Mini, who liked its modern design but added a skylight over an enclosed front patio.

The scale and density of the housing schemes increased somewhat with the completion of Stonebury and Elmhurst in 1960, but the terraces were still only three storeys high. Woodbourne, which was completed in 1963, was noted for its great use of open spaces.[6]

above: **Rear elevation of Beechcroft**

above top: Madin's own house in St Georges Close, from the back
above middle: Nos.1–7 Westbourne Road from Westbourne Gardens
above: The apartment block, Nos.1–7 Westbourne Road

In 1964, Madin's recently completed scheme at Cala Drive and Estria Road won an award from the Ministry of Housing and Local Government. Its awards recognised excellence in housing design and estate layout.

This development consists of two culs-de-sac in the form of an 'L', one leg of which, Cala Drive, is entered from Carpenter Road, and the other, Estria Road, from Wheeleys Road. At the bottom of Cala Drive, a footpath leads into Estria Road with its terraces and two-storey flats, featuring typical Madin recesses for open balconies and porches, grey-buff brick, dark hexagonal tile-hanging and brick piers supporting shiplap timber fascias. The blocks are square, occasionally stepped; the roads and treed lawns curve round them. The influence of Eric Lyons's work for Span is clear, but so too is that of W. Alexander Harvey for the Bournville Tenants Estate.[7]

At the western extremity of the Calthorpe Estate, Madin's low-density style can be seen in the Beech Lanes scheme. Until as late as 1958, this was a large area of virgin land attached to Beech Lane Farm, although it was already encircled by inter-war ribbon housing development and older properties fronting Hagley Road West. This huge 'backland' was originally earmarked for a phased development of 178 houses and 206 flats (160 in multi-storey blocks), and 16 shops. Here, Madin did not have the benefit of mature trees but for the first phase, south of Sir Richards Drive, he devised a large village green around which he deployed a variety of housing types – including a

above top: **The Stonebury and Elmhurst apartments – Norfolk Road, 2005**

above top: Detached and Integro Houses Cala Drive, mid-1960s
above: Madin's Integro Houses Estria Road, 2010

delightful group of single-storey patio houses in Hartford Close, which were completed in 1964.

Clare Drive and Grenfell Drive were completed in 1965, and were described by Douglas Hickman as one of the most attractive groups of houses in the city.[8] The last of the purely low-rise estates was that at Malt Close, a terraced housing scheme in a private cul-de-sac off Metchley Lane completed in 1968.

above top: Patio Houses, Hartford Close, Beech Lanes, 2010
above: Patio of Mr & Mrs Wilson's Hartford Close Home, 2010

above top: Clare and Grenfell Drives from the shared gardens, 2010
above: Clare and Grenfell Drives, interior, 2010

Low- and high-rise together

High Point, West Point and Elmwood Court were the first of the tower-block housing schemes, their concrete frames elegantly clad in brick with long bands of windows and balconies. Unlike much public-sector high-rise housing of this era, they remain in good condition, largely as built in 1961. Each estate consists of a 12–16-storey tower block around which a number of three-storey terraces are set in a mature landscape. They were followed by Chadbrook Crest and Warwick Crest in 1962, using similar designs adapted to the specific conditions of their sites.

The existing trees and landscaping helped to 'swallow' the tower blocks and maintain the character of the area. The blocks are so well sited that they are almost impossible to see from other places, even from high ground on the other side of the Rea Valley. To have achieved such a dramatic transformation without raising the hackles of Edgbaston's residents was a remarkable feat, and shows Madin's skill in producing the discreet modern architecture demanded by his employer.

Madin was not content simply to build housing estates but also included 'village centres' to serve the needs of the residents, which became the hearts of the new neighbourhoods. One local centre, appropriately called Eastern Heart, was completed in 1970

above left: High Point tower, 2010
above right: Warwick Crest tower, 2010

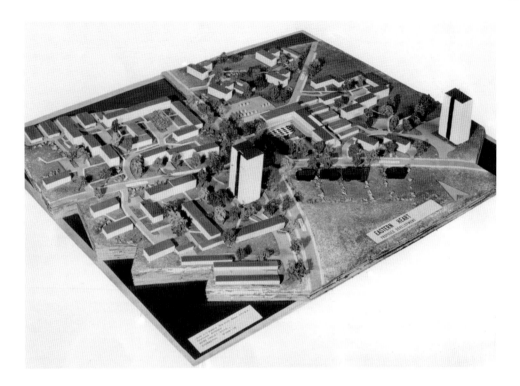

and comprised ten good-quality shop units around Templefield Square, off Wheeleys Road. Its twin, Western Heart, was opened in 1973 at Chad Square, off Harborne Lane near the White Swan public house.

The Calthorpe Estate Commercial Area

There was a shortage of capital in the 1950s, and speculative developers could only expect rents of £75 per square metre (£7 per square foot) per year. Madin offered them simple but elegant rectangular buildings with open floor plans served by a single service core containing stairs, lifts and toilets. The construction industry that Madin had to work with then was not highly skilled, but clients who commissioned buildings for their own use could afford to pay for more expensive and prestigious buildings.

The Calthorpe Estate Commercial Area started modestly with the completion of the low-rise No.100 Hagley Road in 1960. Donne House, a Portland-stone-clad department store for children's outfitter Daniel Neal with offices on two floors, followed in the same year on Calthorpe Road.

above: **The architect's model of the Eastern Heart local centre**

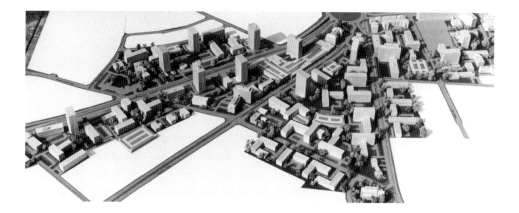

Madin's first large-scale office building on the Calthorpe Estate, the Birmingham Chamber of Commerce at No.75 Harborne Road, was also the first of his buildings to be awarded an RIBA Bronze Medal. Awards given by the Royal Institute of British Architects to its own members carry an extra cachet for architects. The RIBA instituted an annual Bronze Medal in the 1920s for the best London building, and by the post-war period had extended the award to its regions. The programme was remodelled in 1966 to give a greater consistency across the country, with awards for buildings that have high architectural standards and make a significant contribution to the local environment.

As the planning consultant for the Calthorpe Estate, Madin was ideally placed to help his clients with their development proposals and to find suitable sites. The Chamber of Commerce commissioned him in 1955, then realised it could not afford the proposed building straight away; Madin advised his client to extend the site to include a speculative office block, which helped to fund the successful completion of their building in 1960. It was opened by the Duke of Edinburgh on 2 June 1961.

Chamber of Commerce House comprises two blocks at right angles to each other, linked by a set-back shared entrance. The Chamber of Commerce itself originally occupied the lower, four-storey wing, while the larger, eight-storey block was built as offices for letting. The elevations are subtly different, with a greater elaboration used to identify the higher importance of the chamber of commerce block; it uses marbles and Portland stone while the offices are largely clad in aluminium and glass. To mark the opening, the Chamber published a 16-page brochure, lavishly illustrated with Madin's own sketches, showing how the design originated, from overall massing down to curtains, lighting fittings and door handles, and with photographs (including some in colour) of the exterior and interior, including the fittings and furnishings designed or selected by him.

above: The architect's model of the Hagley Road Commercial Area

Although it was on a bigger scale than his previous work, Madin applied the same principles in placing the building in the existing natural landscape. The T-shaped plan allows the landscape to 'wrap around' and mix with the building in a way that would not work with a single, assertive tower, and exemplifies Madin's condition for the

above top: Chamber of Commerce House from Harborne Road, 2010
above right: Chamber of Commerce House exterior, 2010
above left: Mural by John Piper in Chamber of Commerce House

Calthorpe Estate: that no more than a third of any commercial site should be occupied by a building. Inside, Madin enjoyed making spaces. He paid great attention to detail and used different colours of natural stone from distant quarries.

Filmed inside the building for the documentary *Six Men*, Madin said:

> *Architecture is concerned with the organisation of space – the organisation of one space to another. This is the same whether it's inside a building or outside a building, whether it's concerned with the enclosure of space within a group of buildings or enclosure of space within a building. A good example of this is a Gothic church. When you approach the church you go in through a small porch which is low and then you open the doors and walk into the nave. And this gives you this feeling of contrast between the small enclosure of space and a large enclosure of space. And this is what I try to do in a building – to get an interesting movement from one space to another. This is either in the relationship of one room to another, through, say, doors, or an archway, or the relationship of space from one level to another. But you always see buildings through movement. You very rarely stand and look at a building. We are conscious of buildings as we move about, whether it be on foot, or in a motor car. As you walk around an urban area you can feel the space around you. Therefore when an architect designs a comprehensive urban area, he must design this in the scale of movement.*[9]

The entrance hall was originally partly open on the ground floor, allowing pedestrians and vehicles to pass between the two blocks, but since the film was made it has been enclosed. The hall contains a mosaic mural by John Piper, one of only a handful of his works in the genre. Although abstract and geometrical, the mural evokes the impression of blocks of white modern buildings rising from the greens and browns of the old Edgbaston landscape. The building is still in use today and in good condition, but it is threatened by demolition. It is of little consolation that the city council insists that the Piper mural be preserved and given a new home.

Radclyffe House, a low-rise block similar to No.100 Hagley Road, was opened in 1962, and Madin promptly moved his own practice there. The bespoke Shell-Mex House followed in the same year on Calthorpe Road, a neat curtain-walled design again with a low block set against a taller one at right angles. Alexandra Wedgwood noted its 'simple and dignified elevations, with this architect's characteristic use of different materials', and exclaimed, 'What a relief after the London offices of this corporation!'[10] Unfortunately the lake and fountains designed by Madin to satisfy the open-space policy of the Calthorpe Plan have been replaced by car parking, but the green landscaping has matured well. Arthur Thompson House on the Hagley Road was ready for the West Midlands Regional Health Authority to occupy by 1962.

The avenue of offices designed by Madin on Hagley Road brought a modern commercial thrust not just to Edgbaston, but to Birmingham as a whole. Madin's first speculative office tower, Lyndon House, was opened in 1963 on the south side of Hagley Road. The *Six Men* documentary catches the heady atmosphere at the occasion of the

above top: Shell-Mex House, main entrance, c.1962
above: Shell-Mex House, exterior, 2010

opening of its sister, Hagley House (since renamed Cobalt Square), on the opposite side of the Hagley Road in 1965. In the presence of the London property developer, architect and press, the Lord Mayor sets it in a much wider context by saying, 'It's designed in the nicest possible way on an accessible site in a wonderful area and a more wonderful city.'[11] Madin recalls how the female workers from the old city-centre buildings on their first day at Hagley House had worn drab jerseys and thick skirts but on their second day, after they had seen how warm and bright their new offices were, they arrived in summer dresses.

above: Lyndon House with the Portico of Hagley House in the foreground both by Madin, mid-1960s

The last of the rectilinear blocks to be completed, in 1966, was Madin's new headquarters for his practice, No.123 Hagley Road. This was given a Civic Trust Award in 1969, Madin's fourth. Formerly known as Kings House or the John Madin Building, it forms part of a prestigious business location that has seen a revival in recent years.

The building was owned by Madin in conjunction with Norwich Union, and was let to the John Madin Design Group after his retirement in 1975. Madin avoided the use of bare brick in his first office buildings and preferred the purity of plain white surfaces

above: Lyndon House from neighbouring 54 Hagley Road, 2010

which would be self-cleaning. However, with No.123 Hagley Road he turned to brick, Birmingham's traditional building material. It is interesting to see the ancient handcraft of bricklaying combined here with modern concrete-frame construction. Although the bricks themselves were machine-made, the knowledge that they were laid by hand brings a human touch. This is one of Madin's first buildings to suggest Louis Kahn as an influence, seen in the balance of vertical service shafts and columns with the horizontal bands of concrete floors, brickwork and windows – although perhaps the building as a whole is closer to Arup Associates' mineralogy laboratories at Birmingham University, dating from 1964–6.

Belmont House, completed in 1975, saw the emergence of a more complex design style as a result – according to Madin – of improvements in the construction industry

above: John Madin Design Group offices with Beaufort House also by Madin in the background, mid-1970s

and increased commercial-property rental values. A city-council brochure noted how it had 'a sculptural, three-dimensional quality and merge[d] with the landscape by reflecting it and weaving through it'.[12]

Neville House was commissioned in 1972 and completed in 1976, after Madin had retired from practice. It won an RIBA award in 1979 and, with No.54 Hagley Road, marks the culmination of his work in the Calthorpe Estate's commercial area. Its glass skin was a response, says Madin, to a confined site already hemmed in by much taller buildings. By reflecting its surroundings, the building attempts to merge with them instead of vainly competing with them.

The sophisticated dark-tinted glass cladding of Neville House gives it a sense of delicacy and refinement. The public's reaction against the rawness of concrete Brutalism

above: No.123 Hagley Road, exterior, c.1967

was in full flow by 1976, and in lesser hands a reflective façade could have become an abdication from the possibilities of true architecture. This is not the case here, although the glass façade has an impenetrable quality, concealing the interior and the structure of the building – a contrast to the carefully defined bay structures seen in the work of Mies van der Rohe, for example.[13] The completely smooth upper elevations are contrasted with a ground floor recessed behind piers and sitting on a chamfered podium of rough granite setts. The building itself makes no reference to the humanist, Swedish or English modern style found in Madin's early work, but his use of granite setts shows a recurring nostalgia for natural materials hewn and laid by hand.

No.54 Hagley Road, with its subtly irregular façade, was completed in 1978. Since 2000 it has had a prominent new concrete entrance canopy, and is frequently advertised in property supplements as the top-quality, energy-efficient, environmentally friendly flagship of the prestigious Hagley Road business district – proof, if it were needed, of the adaptability and durability of Madin's design. Like Neville House, it remains in excellent condition.

In 1900 the Calthorpe Estate gave land for the relocation of the new University of Birmingham to Edgbaston, and 60 years later the estate leased a nearby site to the BBC

above: **Neville House from Harborne Road, 1976**

so that it could move from a hotchpotch of old city-centre buildings to purpose-built studios, to be known as Pebble Mill, designed by Madin. Alexandra Wedgwood could only judge from the architect's drawings in 1966 when she wrote, 'The whole complex is very carefully planned to obtain the best advantages of its attractive landscape setting.'[14] The ambience of Edgbaston suited BBC people, many of whom moved into Madin-designed houses and apartments.

Madin designed Pebble Mill after studying radio and television studios in the UK and abroad for nine months. It incorporated extensive acoustic and engineering require-ments, and was the first combined radio and television centre anywhere in the world. The glazed entrance hall became the set for the lunchtime chat show *Pebble Mill at One*, while *The Archers'* studio was custom built with its own steps and opening door for sound effects. The buildings were opened by Princess Anne in 1971.

As a result of downsizing, the BBC vacated Pebble Mill in 2004 and moved to The Mailbox in the city centre. The entire complex was demolished in 2005 to make way for a proposed science park that still awaits a developer.

Three higher-education schemes were designed by Madin in Edgbaston. His first commission, completed in 1966, was to refurbish and extend a Victorian mansion,

above: No.54 Hagley Road, 2010

above top: Architect's model of the BBC's Pebble Mill studios
above: Inside a studio of Pebble Mill

Winterbourne, for Birmingham University's Extra-Mural Department. A major new hall of residence, Lucas House, for 150 single and married postgraduate students, was completed in 1967, with Madin selecting a light brick and simple proportions as being most in keeping with the building's residential surroundings.

Between 1961 and 1975, Madin produced a series of schemes for Queen's College, the first ecumenical (multi-denominational) college in the country for training Christian ministers. A hall of residence, a dining block, tutors' accommodation and garages at No.82 Farquhar Road were completed in 1966, followed in 1972 and 1975 by flats, garages, a nursery block and kitchens at Somerset Road.

Edgbaston has always been well endowed with private schools for children of all ages, one of which Madin himself attended as a youngster. Two of these commissioned a variety of projects from him. In the grounds of West House School at No.23 St James Road, Madin added flats for the Head and the housemasters, and a new gymnasium, in 1961–71. For Hallfield School, he built a new classroom, gymnasium, hall, preparatory department, dining room and kitchen in 1967–70, as well as converting a house, No.50 Church Road, to accommodate boarding pupils.

Although just over the northern boundary of the Calthorpe Estate, the Provincial Grand Lodge completed in 1971 for the Warwickshire Lodge of Masons is closely identified with Edgbaston and the Hagley Road. It is now known as the Clarendon Suites (see image p.vi). In *Six Men*, Madin is seen discussing the plans with the client

above: **The main entrance of Pebble Mill, c.2010**

and taking his customary pains to design a building that closely fitted their require-
ments. The result is a most unusual building, mysterious and uncompromising to
passers-by, whose windowless upper floors and fortress-like appearance reinforce the
public image of Freemasonry as a secret society.

A council brochure promoting the best of Birmingham's 1970s buildings notes, 'The
absence of fenestration of the lodge is mitigated by vertical detailing in the brickwork
which sweeps down to form battered buttresses between the ground-floor windows.'
The only concessions to decoration are a concrete parapet and expressive lintels above
the windows. The *Architects' Journal* featured the lodge in a Building Study.[15] More than
30 years after it was built, the building's owners prefer less secrecy and invite the public
to make use of their splendid social facilities.

above: Warwickshire Masonic Temple, 2010

Madin's Edgbaston legacy

Madin had so subtly modernised the old Calthorpe family estate by the late 1970s that those who knew it before had hardly noticed what had happened. The city council made virtually all of the eastern half a Conservation Area in 1975.[16] The housing estates designed by Madin in Edgbaston have not inspired an urban folklore like their contemporary counterparts, the big council estates. Lynsey Hanley, who was brought up in Alan Maudsley's Chelmsley Wood, tells of its isolation, drabness and suffocating social uniformity.[17] Madin's Egbaston presents a very different picture, although, like its largely middle-class population, it had a much better start in life than Chelmsley Wood. Not only was it close to the amenities of the city centre, it was blessed with mature landscape that was never likely to be destroyed by large uniform estates of council housing.

above: Warwickshire Masonic Temple, view of inner hall, 2010

Madin became aware by the late 1960s that the success of his Calthorpe Estate housing had paved the way for other developers who were less committed to his design precepts and the values enshrined in his plan. He felt his position had become untenable when land at Berrow Hall was sold to volume housebuilders Bryants, and Sir Richard Calthorpe – with whom he had worked so successfully – relinquished his day-to-day control over the estate. After the latter's death in 1985, it became clear that his son and successor, Sir Euan Hamilton Anstruther-Gough-Calthorpe, was less personally committed to the ideals that underpinned his father's partnership with Madin.

This departure from the planning and design principles laid down in the original plan was accompanied by a proposed demolition of one of its centrepieces. In 2000, the Chamber of Commerce, encouraged by a commercial property developer and supported by the City planners, sought to replace Madin's building with a new, bigger office block. The policy adopted in the 1957–8 master plan is now seen by the Calthorpe Estate as too restrictive, as it prevents the entire footprint of a site being built on. The value of land has increased to the point where amenity landscape around a building is under great economic pressure. Not only is the future of Chamber of Commerce House in question, but the abandonment of the plot-ratio policy in this case will set a precedent for others to follow and will lead, in Madin's view, to more of the planning 'chaos' that he sees in the city centre. As of 2010 the Chamber's plans are on hold, but their existence indicates the huge financial pressure arising from increasing land values in what has become one of the most desirable commercial locations in Birmingham.

The comprehensive planning and design of entire communities lies closest to Madin's heart. In this respect, he was to be disappointed at the way in which his founding principles were later ignored or watered down – owing, he felt, to a failure of nerve by the Calthorpe Estate in resisting pressure from speculative house-builders and developers. However, all has not been lost: the estate still tries to maintain its character by requiring its leaseholders to sign up to a 13-page 'Scheme of Management' enacted under the Leasehold Reform Act of 1967, and despite difficulties of enforcement it has been largely successful. The Edgbaston Conservation Area should protect not only the traditional buildings but also the modern ones designed by Madin. Apart from Pebble Mill, Donne House and his own home, Madin's Edgbaston legacy is surviving well at present and can be seen as the foundation of his architectural and planning practice.

Notes

1. Readers wishing to get the feel for the classic character of the area, both past and present, are recommended to follow the walking tour in Andy Foster, *Pevsner Architectural Guides: Birmingham*, 2005, pp212–39.

2. *An Introduction to the Calthorpe Estate Redevelopment Proposals*, 1958, p24. Madin is not named as 'the architect' in the booklet, but the words sound like his. There is also a double-page spread of the zoning plan, and some anonymous architectural sketches.

3. *Window on Edgbaston* was published by Calthorpe Estates as an A4 booklet to accompany the 1962 exhibition. It was written by Hilary Millward, with freehand sketches and maps prepared by John H. D. Madin & Partners and photographs by Cecil Reilly.

4. Nikolaus Pevsner, *An Outline of European Architecture*, 1942, pp433–5.

5. Philip Smith, 'Architect joins house fight. Extension "would ruin prototype"', *Birmingham Post*, 20 June 1990.

6. Nikolaus Pevsner and Alexandra Wedgwood, *The Buildings of England, Warwickshire*, 1966, p173.

7. Foster, *op. cit.*, pp228–9.

8. Douglas Hickman, *Birmingham*, 1970, pp74–6. Hickman, a former partner of Madin's, was Birmingham's leading architectural historian until his untimely death in 1990.

9. John Madin speaking in René Cutforth, *Six Men*, 1962.

10. Pevsner and Wedgwood, *op. cit.*, p173.

11. Birmingham's Lord Mayor, Councillor Frank Price, speaking at the opening of Hagley House in Cutforth, *op.cit.*

12. Birmingham City Council Planning Department, *70s Birmingham Buildings*, 1997, unpag.

13. Foster, *op. cit.*, pp221–2.

14. Pevsner and Wedgwood, *op. cit.*, p175.

15. *Architects' Journal*, 5 March 1972, pp497–510.

16. Birmingham City Council, *Edgbaston Conservation Area No. 15*. It was designated in 1975, and extended in 1984 and 1992 – 395.3 hectares (976.9 acres).

17. Lynsey Hanley, *Estates – an intimate history*, 2007.

3 Commerce and industry

It would be surprising to find an architect born, trained and based in the great manufacturing city of Birmingham who did not work for commercial and industrial clients, both there and beyond. Madin established connections early on with both sides of industry – as well as with the banking, utilities and communications sectors – and his work for these clients is among his very best. In time, his commercial work extended well beyond his base in Hagley Road and the Calthorpe Estate. By 1965 this work was at its peak, and Madin's was presented in *Six Men* as a largely commercial firm.[1]

The first commissions from the business community came in 1954 from Englands, a Wigan-based chain of shoe shops that expanded in two years with the opening of 17 stores in the Midlands and the North of England. The designs were proof, in Madin's view, of the popular appeal of the 'modern open façade stretching across the whole width of the property facing the High Street'.[2] The first Englands shop boasted an innovative flight of open-tread stairs to its first-floor ladies' department, but Madin recalls that the managers felt that the ladies would be embarrassed using them so they moved their department to the ground floor and put the men on the first floor instead. At the same time, Madin was employed designing 15 Sweeney Radio shops and half a dozen drapery shops for Yarnolds in the West Midlands. These designs were very modern additions to the traditional high street. Englands, Sweeney Radios and Yarnolds have all since disappeared as brands, and the shops have gone with them.

opposite: Broadway and No.1 Hagley Road as viewed from Broad Street
above: An Englands shoe shop, Standishgate Wigan, c.1955

An early commercial town-planning scheme was a master plan for the Ladywell Centre in Birmingham, in 1959. Madin was asked to design a comprehensive entertainment and shopping centre covering 4.6 hectares (11.5 acres) near the city centre, on land owned by the ancient Gooch Estate. The brief was for shops, a cinema, dance hall, ice rink, bowling alley, leisure centre, flats and a multi-storey car park. The only part of the plan realised – the Silver Blades Ice Rink designed by Gillinson & Barnett and opened in 1964 – is now in a very sad state of repair. Its derelict state today contrasts starkly with contemporary projects on the Calthorpe Estate where Madin was an integral part of the development process.

The Amalgamated Engineering Union commissioned Madin to design its new offices and an 800-seat assembly room at Holloway Circus, a project that was completed in 1961. Clearly he was trusted by both sides of industry at a time when relations between them were often difficult. This was a three-storey building on an awkward corner site turning into Holloway Circus, with shops at ground level and projecting canopies above. Andy Foster remembers it as boasting 'an elegant, deceptively simple façade of glazed panels and thin concrete mullions and a recessed balcony'.[3] A full-height open staircase was supported on flying bridges and a single column. Around the year 2000 the union received an offer for the site, and the building was demolished in 2005 to make way for the 40-storey Radisson Hotel.

In Broad Street, also in the city centre, a nine-storey office block, Granville House, was opened in 1963. It was clumsily re-clad around 1990 as a Travelodge, but it is testament to the building's adaptability that it could be put to an entirely new use. Broadgate House, later Rail House and now named Quayside Tower, was built in 1966 on Broad Street as a mixed comprehensive development that included offices, a control centre and a staff restaurant for British Rail, plus shops and a multi-storey car park. The low 'podium' block follows the pattern set by Skidmore Owings and Merrill's Lever House in New York, opened in 1952, but here Madin gave the formula added interest with the commissioning of a series of sculptured concrete panels from William Mitchell.[4] The office tower was re-clad in 2003 by Richard Johnson and Associates. Since Broad Street became Birmingham's main nightclub area, it has appeared to float serenely above the pubs and bars jostling below.

In 1964, Madin completed a 7,400-square metre (80,000-square foot) office building in Smethwick for the old-established metal window manufacturer Henry Hope & Sons. The company had designed and made the Terrace Glasshouses of 1884 in Birmingham's Botanical Gardens, close to Madin's home and office. His project represented the first part of a three-phase programme for the rebuilding of the company's offices and, Madin explained, the 12-month building programme had to be planned very exactly to maintain continuity of production. The cladding, specially developed by Hope's, represented a breakthrough in design, for the usual solid fire-check backup wall was omitted, and it featured in the *Architects' Journal*.[5] The building is still in use today.

above top left: Rail House (Quayside Tower), c.1966
above top right: A concrete panel by sculptor William Mitchell, Rail House, 2010
above left: Henry Hope's offices, Smethwick, exterior view, c.1965
above right: Henry Hope's offices, staircase detail, 2010

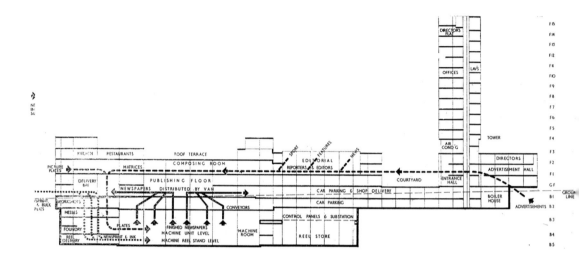

Glass curtain walls of the kind which Madin used at Henry Hope featured again in the tower block for the *Birmingham Post and Mail*, designed in 1961 and opened in 1966. Here, Madin's task was to integrate a printing works, newspaper complex and commercial offices into a coherent group of buildings on a restricted city-centre site.

This development was marked by another tower and podium. The highlights were the split-level entrance in the podium and the adjoining advertising hall at the foot of the tower, where the public could come and place their entries for the classified sections. The podium was planned imaginatively to house all the principal functions of a newspaper business of the time – a composing room, type store and editorial room – in large open-plan spaces, surrounded by smaller editorial offices. Dining and recreational facilities were set above, around an open roof terrace. The podium was clad in glass, marble, black granite stone and large-aggregate terrazzo, while the 17-storey tower block was faced in dark grey glass with aluminium mullions, and its upper floors were let commercially. The podium was linked to the printing works, which by contrast was dark, clad in stone and bush-hammered concrete with pre-cast concrete louvres. Foster thought it 'the best 1960s commercial building in Birmingham ... the gentle 1950s manner replaced by something tougher and of national interest'.[6] The plan of the podium was C-shaped, forming a courtyard, with the cornice carried dramatically across the open side on piers as an open arcade.

above: Cross section through the *Birmingham Post and Mail* Building

above: *Birmingham Post and Mail* Building, Colmore Circus, c.1970

By 2000, printing machinery had become more compact and regional newspapers were in decline owing to the rapid growth of electronic media in publishing. The building was turned down for listing in 2002, as architects on English Heritage's advisory committee of outside experts were unhappy with the abrupt junction between

above top: The *Post and Mail* tower taken shortly before it wa demolished
above: *Post and Mail* advertisement hall, c.1970

the light and dark portions of the building, one of the characteristic features of Madin's work that makes it so dramatic. The tower and podium were subsequently demolished so that the site could be redeveloped more intensively. In 2009, the *Post and Mail* moved its entire operation to the refurbished Fort Dunlop, leaving the printing hall at Colmore Circus empty and itself ripe for development.

Another building by Madin to win a Civic Trust Award (in 1969) was his Midlands regional office for the Central Electricity Generating Board (CEGB) in Solihull, built in 1961–7. As with many of his buildings, he softened the development's overall bulk by breaking it down into several blocks of different heights and sizes, and reflected their different functions with subtle variations of materials and styles. The main administrative block is eight storeys high and has a gentle convex curve on both of its long sides, but a concave curve on both of its short sides. In contemporary photographs, the horizontal bands of windows avoid monotony by incorporating a random pattern of light-coloured screens or blinds inside. The projecting ventilation ducts on the building's main façades were added later. The three-storey block and the lower, welfare building make a marked contrast with the main block, and the complex 'floats' in a mature landscape. Since the CEGB was abolished the buildings have stood empty, and the site is now owned by the Asda retail chain. Proposals to demolish them and build a supermarket on the site awaited approval in early 2011.

above: Central Electricity Generating Board, Solihull, c.1968

Madin had, by 1960, established a dignified commercial modern style that was acceptable to prestigious clients such as high-street banks. His first job for Barclays Bank was to fit out a branch in the new office block at No.106 Hagley Road in 1961. There followed 15 more branches, some of which were small-scale fit-out jobs while others were entirely new buildings. The best examples, boasting well-preserved glass curtain walls with stainless steel or aluminium mullions, can still be seen at Northfield, Sparkhill, Shirley and Wolverhampton. After Barclays moved out of its Snow Hill branch, the building was given a new lease of life as a Citizens Advice Bureau in 2007 – a clear indication both of the changing pattern of high-street banking and the commercial decline of the traditional high street itself. A small number of similar commissions were carried out for the National Westminster Bank, Martins Bank, Lloyds Bank and the District Bank.

In Coventry, a 16-storey headquarters office block for Massey Ferguson was completed in 1966, but it is disappointing compared with the elegant curtain walling and curved façade, reminiscent of London's Millbank Tower, that Madin had shown in his design perspectives. The company was acquired by Agco in 1995, who vacated the office building in September 2006. The surrounding buildings, not designed by Madin, have since been demolished, leaving the tower isolated.

above: **Barclays Bank, Wolverhampton, c.1970**

above: **The two towers of Coventry Point, mid-1970s**

Madin's Brutalist phase can be seen at its most full-blooded in the National Westminster Bank and its related office development, opened in 1974 in central Birmingham. As one of the most monumental office buildings in the city, it disregards some planning conventions but had, as Foster noted, a 'tremendous integrity' all its own.[7] This astonishing 20-storey structure was built in the Colmore Row Conservation Area, overtopping Edwardian and Victorian neighbours such as the former Eagle Insurance Offices of 1900 by Lethaby and Ball. Although the NatWest was a large project, it was broken up into a number of units as was the Madin custom, in an approach similar to that adopted by Alison and Peter Smithson in their development for *The Economist* in London. An earlier NatWest scheme by Madin from 1964 owes something to Louis Kahn's laboratories for the University of Pennsylvania, the main phase of which was completed in 1960.

Like the Smithsons' development, Madin's design respects the scale of the traditional street by setting the main tower behind lower blocks that maintain the street line and height of their neighbours. The complex is clad in pre-cast concrete panels that have a very rough aggregate finish, each of which frames a window. Plum-coloured Staffordshire engineering bricks clad service towers that soar well above the tops of the office blocks. The ensemble is quintessentially Brutalist, and turns an industrial

above left: The banking hall of the National Westminster Bank, c.1972
above right: The front doors by sculptor William Mitchell, 2010

above top left: National Westminster Bank and Tower from Victoria Square, 2010
above right: National Westminster Bank and Tower from Colmore Row, c.1975
above left: National Westminster Bank and Tower from Colmore Row, 2010

building into something romantic and full of drama, which when abandoned by its human occupants was adopted as a remote cliff top by a peregrine falcon which built its nest there.

The interior was enlivened by abstract murals and bronze matt ceramic tiles, and the concrete coffered ceiling of the public banking hall was lined with gold leaf. Bronze-effect doors, designed by William Mitchell, incorporate geometric shapes that refer abstractly to the National Westminster Bank logo. In 1997, Birmingham City Council published a brochure highlighting the best of the city's 1970s architecture, in which the National Westminster Bank was admired for its 'severity and cool'. The banking hall still retained many original features, including light fittings and 'sweeping teak window cills'.[8]

Twenty years after it was opened, however, the city council decided that the bank did not look right alongside the neo-classical Council House and the other Victorian buildings in Colmore Row. With the encouragement of the city planners, one of the lower blocks facing Colmore Row was replaced in 1996–7 by a building from the Seymour Harris Partnership that attempted to replicate the historical streetscape. The remodelling may have been well intentioned, but it made a nonsense of the original design. Following this partial mutilation of Madin's design, the city planners have since sanctioned its complete demolition, to be replaced by a 35-storey glass tower rising from the street-front boundary of the site – a questionable response to its neo-classical context. Even after the 1990s modifications, the Madin building is worth keeping. The redevelopment is on hold in the economic downturn of 2009–11. In a climate that now favours pragmatic refurbishment, the remodelling of Madin's contemporary No.54 Hagley Road as part of the 'renaissance' of the Hagley Road Business District shows what can be done.

West Bromwich town centre

Madin's master plan for this redevelopment of a traditional high street comprised two phases of an enclosed shopping centre, or mall, the first of which became known as Queen's Square. René Cutforth, in *Six Men*, described West Bromwich town centre as 'a typically squalid relic of the industrial blitz'.[9] In the film, Madin introduces the project by saying:

> Once the golden mile, the High Street of West Bromwich is now completely choked with traffic. Surrounded by obsolete buildings. Surrounded by some derelict land. Life in the centre is frustrating and dangerous. In one year there were 96 road accidents in the town centre alone. This is a situation most of our industrial cities face today. And for the doubters who believe that full-scale comprehensive redevelopment of our town centres is just a planner's dream, it has been shown at West Bromwich that the citizens of the town can redevelop their town centre and this is both feasible and

*practical and it can be done at a price that they can afford – a two-penny-
halfpenny rate or about fivepence a week for the average ratepayer. And for
this price the heart of West Bromwich will be re-created as a pleasant town
centre where the citizens may live, relax, and enjoy their leisure hours as
well as shop and work.*

The centre is encircled by a gyratory road system that gives access to the bus station
and to free car parks. The first phase of the master plan, consisting of an air-conditioned
shopping centre, bus interchange and multi-storey car park, was a joint development by
West Bromwich County Borough Council and the National Coal Board Mineworkers'
Pension Fund. It was opened in 1971 by the Chairman of the National Coal Board,
Derek Ezra. During the design stage, Madin had to persuade cautious councillors to
accept a mall of the kind he had seen on a recent visit to the United States. He planned
the development so that people would have to pass the shops, including Marks and
Spencer, when walking between the new bus station or car park and the High Street.
The second phase, King's Square, was opened in 1974. It consists of an air-conditioned
shopping centre and market hall, and was a joint development by French Kier Property
Investments Limited and the borough council. The central octagonal space has since
been remodelled, but the rest is much as designed.

Even inside a closed shopping centre in the heart of the Black Country, Madin
provided pools and fountains to humanise the modern surroundings and give harassed

above: The water feature in Queen's Square, West Bromwich centre, c.1975

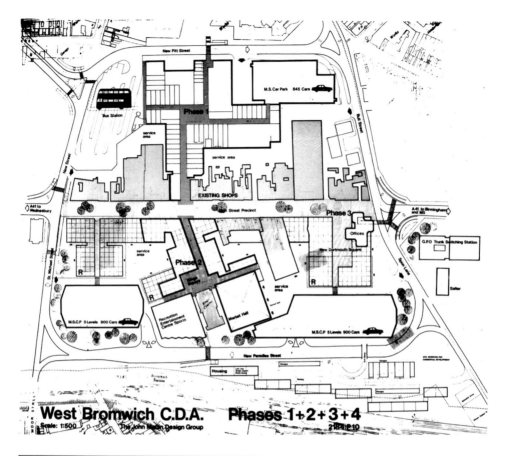

above top: The master plan for West Bromwich centre
above: King's Square, West Bromwich, c.1975

shoppers a relaxing non-mechanical light-and-sound show, an idea that was to reappear beneath and around Birmingham's Central Library. The fountains have since been boarded over, sadly, but otherwise both centres have prospered. However, the local authority (since 1974 the Metropolitan Borough of Sandwell) has plans to redevelop the town centre that may affect Madin's work.

Within walking distance of Queen's Square is the Lyng Regeneration Zone, in which can be found Madin's little Church of the Good Shepherd, opened in 1968. Just beyond the gyratory road stands his police headquarters, completed in 1972 but now looking very unloved.

The shift in architectural taste that became evident in the 1960s from glass-and-aluminium curtain walls to concrete Brutalism is exemplified by the *Yorkshire Post* Building in Leeds. The chairman of its sister paper, the *Birmingham Post and Mail*, recommended Madin for the job in 1964. The building was opened by Prince Charles in 1970, and awarded the RIBA's Bronze Medal in 1971.[10]

Madin's characteristically modernist preference for breaking up large projects into clearly identifiable parts is seen again in this design. A three-storey block connects a six-storey slab with a blank-walled octagonal block on stilts, which dominates a busy street corner and forms the complex's defining landmark. Behind it, the motif of the freestanding service tower is used twice. Otherwise it is a building very different from Madin's remaining oeuvre, with greater similarities to low-rise office slabs of the 1970s such as the Building Design Partnership's offices for the Halifax Building Society (1972–4). The *Yorkshire Post* Building bears no visible human marks, not even brickwork, and when it was completed it sat on a bleak corner in a northern industrial

above: The *Yorkshire Post* Building from above, c.1975

above top: The *Yorkshire Post* Building today, 2010
above: Main reception, *Yorkshire Post* Building, c.1971

city. The young trees, planted as part of the scheme, are hardly visible in the contemporary photograph against the towering mass of the building.

What were the qualities that led the RIBA to award the building its Bronze Medal? Clearly it was thought of as a ground-breaking and outstanding achievement. It is architects' architecture, but it was also practical. The RIBA assessors – Kenneth Campbell, James Gowan and Geoffrey Davey – wrote:

> *From the Client's point of view this building appears to be an extremely successful solution to their very complex planning problem. The production of a major national daily newspaper, as well as an important evening paper, encompasses a very wide range of activities of [an] extremely varied nature ... On an awkward site, bounded by a canal and a major roadway intersection, and surrounded by a changing backcloth of unplanned but almost heroic vigour, the building both by day and night makes a dramatic contribution.*[11]

The strong design was the result of Madin's painstaking research and attention to every detail of the client's needs. The people of Leeds, however, must have thought that an alien spaceship had landed in their city. We can see architectural features that were to reappear in the Birmingham Central Library a few years later, including the cruciform concrete columns, coffered ceilings and deep concrete balconies.

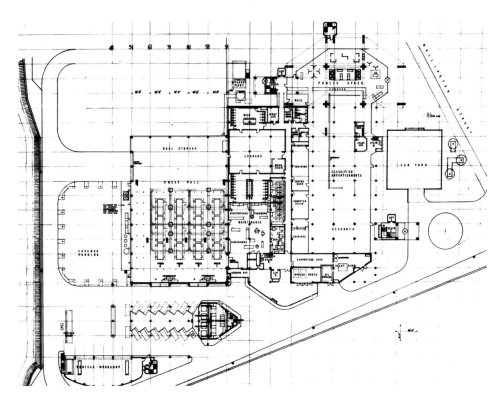

above: **Floor plan of the *Yorkshire Post* Building**

Dominating Birmingham's Five Ways, Metropolitan House was completed in 1974 and illustrates the later, more complex style adopted by Madin and his partners. According to Madin, the client was prepared to finance a higher-quality product than the practice's earlier office buildings in order to enhance the company's reputation and to take advantage of the increased rent obtainable in the late 1960s and improvements in the quality of construction.[12] Instead of a rectangular block, this is a faceted

above: Metropolitan House (No.1 Hagley Road) Fiveways, 2010

and highly modulated one. Moreover, it occupies much more of its site than do Madin's early blocks, for instance on the Calthorpe Estate, reflecting its position closer to the city centre. The lower-rise Broadway development at Five Ways was completed in 1976, and is denoted by a striking central service tower, from which faceted blocks of various sizes and shapes radiate.

A new operational headquarters for the Automobile Association in Halesowen was also completed in 1974. This immaculately designed suite of buildings was constructed when the Association relocated from Birmingham's Hagley Road. It was the clearest expression of Madin's characteristic brick architecture. Since 2007, it has stood empty and vandalised although it is within sight of a town centre that is undergoing regeneration. It is another example of a purpose-built corporate headquarters being abandoned because of a changed business environment.

Madin also worked in the nearby city of Coventry, whose centre was rebuilt even more comprehensively than Birmingham's after the war. The twin white towers of Coventry Point, completed in 1975, can easily be seen from the railway station as they rise dramatically from the heart of the city above the intervening trees. They depart from the rectilinear Calthorpe Estate office blocks, although the horizontal bands of windows and white walls hark back to them. The bulky development is characteristically broken down into smaller parts.

above: The Broadway office complex, Five Ways, 2010

In Northfield, on the southern edge of Birmingham, Madin designed phase two of the Grosvenor Shopping Centre next to the existing phase one by another architect. It was opened in 1975, and is still in good condition and commercially successful. Madin's design deals with the problem of the blank exterior of shopping malls by

above: The Automobile Association in Halesowen, shortly after completion, c.1975

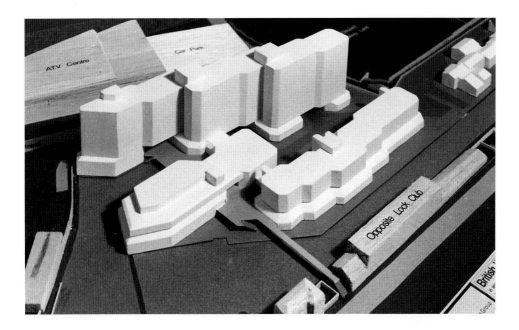

using strongly modelled brown brickwork panels. The parapet rails of the flat roof are supported between little concrete pillars bearing low-relief medallions. The style that Madin developed for an earlier blank-walled building, the Provincial Grand Masonic Lodge in Edgbaston, was clearly brought to bear again here.

A plan for Worcester Bar in the Gas Street area of Birmingham was commissioned in 1973 by the British Waterways Board, which was looking to develop its freehold interests. Both sides of Broad Street had become rather run-down and detached from the city centre since the 1950s, and the city council had mooted various proposals for its redevelopment. The economic downturn that followed in the late 1970s meant that the plans, published in 1975, were not realised.

Interspersed with Madin's Midlands commissions during the 1970s were several overseas projects, including a small office block in Amman in Jordan; a commercial and residential development in Libya; and a large 'twin tower' office development in Sharjah, part of the United Arab Emirates. The resulting office blocks are similar to No.54 Hagley Road in their use of pre-cast concrete cladding panels.

As a result of his work for the BBC at Pebble Mill, Madin was appointed by the major electronics company Marconi in 1970 to design a suite of new television and radio studios for a site in Zagreb, then part of the Socialist Federal Republic of Yugoslavia and now the capital of Croatia. The design was then handed over to the state broadcasting corporation, who employed local architects to supervise its construction in 1975. At the

above: Architect's model of the Worcester Bar Development

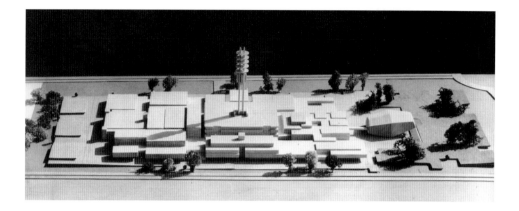

time Yugoslavia was a communist state, and Madin recalls finding out that his hotel room had been 'bugged' – his client already knew what he had discussed with Marconi the day before they met. The centre was built substantially as designed, was taken over by Croatian Radio Television after the dissolution of Yugoslavia and is still used for its original purpose. Madin has confirmed that his original design is still clearly recognisable.

Given the quantity of commercial work carried out by the Madin office, it is unsurprising that it has been widely perceived as a purely commercial practice. This was not altogether justified, as this book shows elsewhere, but it was understandable because of the high visibility and impressiveness of the commercial buildings compared with the retiring quality of Madin's housing schemes for the Calthorpe Estate or the unglamorous products of the new towns. Commercial clients wanted the world to see how successful they were, and Madin's buildings elegantly expressed the boundless confidence in the future that was widely held at the time.

above: Architect's model of Yugoslavia TV & Radio station

Notes

1. René Cutforth, narrating the BBC2 documentary series *Six Men* in 1965, comments that 'the name of John Madin up to now has been associated with the demands of the opulent client, whether individuals or company. When you see his name on the board it will probably be near a main shopping street.'

2. Conversation between John Madin and the author, April 2010.

3. Andy Foster, *Pevsner Architectural Guides: Birmingham*, 2005, p200.

4. William George Mitchell (b.1925) was a prolific sculptor in concrete and bronze-effect fibreglass, initially for the London County Council and then in private practice. Examples of his relief sculpture feature at a number of listed buildings, including Liverpool and Clifton Roman Catholic Cathedrals, and Harrod's store in Knightsbridge. Individual works by Mitchell are listed: Wexham Springs (the former Cement and Concrete Association), the Three Tuns public house in Coventry, and Harlow Water Gardens.

5. *Architects' Journal*, 2 December 1964, pp1319–21.

6. Foster, *op. cit.*, pp30–1.

7. Foster, *op. cit.*, pp95–7.

8. Birmingham City Council's Planning Department produced a series of illustrated brochures in 1992–7, one of which was *70s Birmingham Buildings*, 1997. It is interesting to see that council officers considered Madin's buildings worthy of high praise in 1997, shortly before councillors started making unfavourable comments about some of them. Five of the eight buildings featured in the brochure were designed by Madin – Belmont House, the Central Reference Library, National Westminster Bank, Neville House and the 'Warwickshire Masonic Temple' (the Provincial Grand Masonic Lodge described in Chapter 2).

9. Cutforth, *op. cit.* His words are accompanied by grim black-and-white shots of knots of anxious-looking people, struggling to cross a high street choked with buses and lorries.

10. Prince Charles was not at this time an outspoken critic of modernist buildings as he was to become following his speech at the RIBA Gold Medal Award in May 1984.

11. *RIBA Journal*, August 1971, pp341–52.

12. Conversation between John Madin and the author, April 2010.

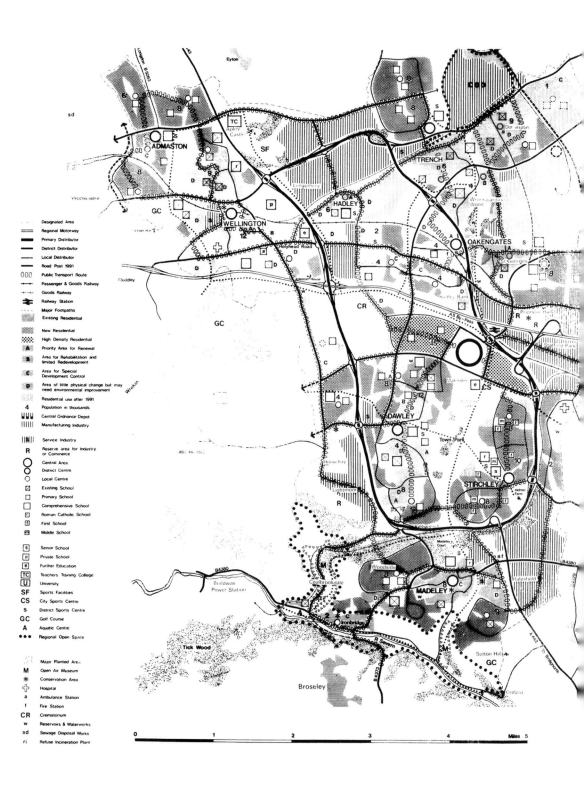

Designated Area

Regional Motorway

Primary Distributor

District Distributor

Local Distributor

Road Post 1991

Public Transport Route

Passenger & Goods Railway

Goods Railway

Railway Station

Major Footpaths

Existing Residential

New Residential

High Density Residential

Priority Area for Renewal

Area for Rehabilitation and limited Redevelopment

Area for Special Development Control

Area of little physical change but may need environmental improvement

Residential use after 1991

4   Population in thousands

Central Ordnance Depot

Manufacturing Industry

Service Industry

R   Reserve area for Industry or Commerce

Central Area

District Centre

Local Centre

Existing School

Primary School

Comprehensive School

Roman Catholic School

First School

Middle School

S   Senior School

P   Private School

e   Further Education

TC   Teachers Training College

U   University

SF   Sports Facilities

CS   City Sports Centre

s   District Sports Centre

GC   Golf Course

A   Aquatic Centre

•••   Regional Open Space

Major Planted Area

M   Open Air Museum

✳   Conservation Area

✛   Hospital

a   Ambulance Station

f   Fire Station

CR   Crematorium

w   Reservoirs & Waterworks

sd   Sewage Disposal Works

ri   Refuse Incineration Plant

0   1   2   3   4   Miles 5

4   New places

The experience of being the master planner and architect for the Calthorpe Estate had given Madin a crash course in the art of planning large housing developments, shopping centres, whole neighbourhoods and new towns for people he would never meet. In the 1950s, learning on the job was an important way of mastering town-planning skills. There were few experienced and qualified professional town planners around, for although Liverpool ran a town-planning course from the 1900s the first in London began only in the 1930s; Birmingham did not have a School of Planning until 1959. But when the opportunity presented itself to assist the government with its new towns programme, Madin was ready and able to start straight away. His skills and knowledge were also of great interest to private property developers, both in the UK and abroad, and he was quick to grow this side of his practice.

As Michael Barker and Graham Reddie recall, 'Re-housing Birmingham people had already begun under the Town Development Act of 1952 at Dawley, where 100 dwellings were provided between 1958 and 1961'.[1] Dawley was a small Shropshire town of 22,000 people some 65 kilometres (40 miles) north-west of Birmingham and close to Ironbridge Gorge, birthplace of the Industrial Revolution. However, the 1952 Act was slow to administer and provided no opportunity for comprehensive planning, something needed in an area scarred with the obsolete remains and abandoned spoil heaps from long-gone coal-mining and iron-founding industries. The government had rejected an expansion plan by Birmingham City Council in 1960, but a year later it started to review its policies towards new towns, and the Midlands New Town Society's campaign for one in the West Midlands began to receive serious consideration.

Madin was brought into contact with central government on this issue thanks to the 'Window on Edgbaston' exhibition, which was opened by the Junior Minister for Housing, Lord Jellicoe, in 1962.[2] Madin recalls that Keith Joseph, who had just been made Minister of Housing by the Macmillan Government with a brief to mount the biggest slum-clearance programme of all time, then asked to meet him to discuss the expansion of Corby New Town. He was clearly impressed by Madin's work in Edgbaston. Having refused to create more new towns following their election victory in 1951, save for Cumbernauld, the Conservatives now launched a second wave of designations, which was continued by the Labour governments after 1964. The meeting with Madin eventually led to commissions for Dawley and Telford new towns. Madin had already started to assemble a team to undertake the major planning jobs that followed in quick succession in the early 1960s, as the new town programme was announced and city-centre redevelopment gathered pace.

opposite: **Madin's master plan for Telford New Town**

Madin was commissioned in 1962 to carry out a feasibility study for the Ministry of Housing and Local Government on the cost implication of expanding Worcester to receive overspill population from Birmingham, while other firms of consultants undertook studies of Peterborough and Ipswich. Madin's brief required an examination of the physical, social and cost implications of 50 per cent and 100 per cent population increases over time-frames of either 15 or 25 years, which would have meant a maximum population for Worcester of 130,000. A report on the proposals was published by the Government in 1964, but its recommendations were not adopted, and the population of Worcester grew more slowly to the figure of 95,000 today.

Corby New Town

Madin's first major town-planning commission was to draw up a revised master plan for Corby, incorporating the existing development. Designated as one of the first wave of post-war new towns in 1950, Corby needed to expand in line with the growing workforce of Stewart and Lloyds' steelworks. By 1963, when Madin was appointed, its population of 40,000 was set to rise to 75,000.

The plan that Madin drew up for Corby was sensible and down-to-earth. The new element in town planning in 1965, absent as late as 1950 when William Holford and Myles Wright had prepared the first plan for the town, was the domination of the automobile. Cars, lorries, vans and buses demanded sweeping curves and multilevel junctions. A new breed of highway engineers dictated turning circles, sight lines, gradients, widths and construction according to the speed, size and function of the predicted traffic. The architect-planners were left with the task of allocating the correct number, type and location of houses, shops, schools, factories and other facilities within this prescribed structure, while the physical boundary was tightly defined by the government. Master planners who were also architects, such as Madin, were sometimes asked to design residential neighbourhoods, industrial estates or town-centre buildings but, as in the late 1940s, most building work was handed over to the new town corporation's own salaried architect's department or to private developers.

The master plan for the redesign and expansion of Corby town centre was published in 1965. The shopping centre planned from 1950 still exists today and its Festival of Britain style has considerable period charm, but its main thoroughfare, Corporation Street, was originally open to traffic – something quite unfashionable by the 1960s. Today, it is fascinating to see three distinct architectural and planning phases – the 1930s, 1950s and 1960s – side by side as if exposed by an archaeological dig. However, Madin was not involved in designing the individual buildings in the central area.

The Brookside housing estate in Corby was completed in 1967 to Madin's design. It comprised Northbrook, Highbrook, Southbrook and Kingsbrook off Colyers Avenue, and Eastbrook off Gainsborough Road. Routes for pedestrians and vehicles were separated by the houses, in the manner first developed at Radburn, New Jersey, and which was the preferred planning option in the 1960s. The distinctive features of the

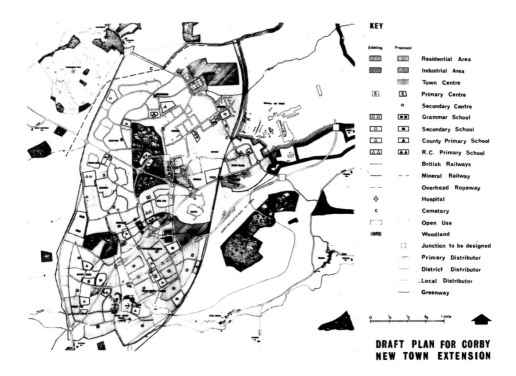

KEY

Existing	Proposed	
		Residential Area
		Industrial Area
		Town Centre
S	S	Primary Centre
	□	Secondary Centre
		Grammar School
		Secondary School
		County Primary School
		R.C. Primary School
		British Railways
		Mineral Railway
		Overhead Ropeway
		Hospital
c		Cemetary
		Open Use
		Woodland
		Junction to be designed
		Primary Distributor
		District Distributor
		Local Distributor
		Greenway

**DRAFT PLAN FOR CORBY
NEW TOWN EXTENSION**

above top: The Corby master plan for New Town Extension
above: Architect's model of the Corby Town Centre

housing are the hipped roofs of the three-storey dwellings and the concrete balconies on the two-storey units – the latter big enough to accommodate, in one case, a small greenhouse. The estate has survived better than the larger and more densely developed Canada Estate to the south. The main alteration undergone since completion has been the closing of the pedestrian throughways as an anti-crime measure, a change that has made it impossible to walk freely through the estate as originally intended. Much of the open landscape of the pedestrian courts has been privatised, with little wooden fences erected as part of the move for more 'defensible space' in the 1980s and 1990s.

above: Sketch of proposed Corby town centre

above top: Plan of Brookside, Corby New Town
above: Housing at Brookside, Corby, c.1967

Telford New Town

Madin was also appointed in 1963 to design the new town of Dawley, and in 1965 he presented his plan to a public meeting which was filmed by the BBC.[3] Addressing a crowded village hall, he described in his measured and eloquent manner his feelings for the place:

> During a very concentrated year, Dawley's designated area has lost none of its initial impact and excitement which it had on me when I first saw this area. And I believe we have an opportunity here to create one of the finest industrial towns not only in this country but in the world. And I think I can say this because I have seen most of the major developments of this kind in the Western world. The New Town has an area of 9,168 acres ... bounded by the A5 bypass on the north, the Severn Gorge to the south and boundaries of about two and a half miles apart on the east and west. Within the central area there are a number of possible locations for a main centre, adjacent to the beautiful Randlay Lake. The valley site offers the opportunity of development as a multi-level centre by making use of part of the Randlay Valley. The servicing and storage of the town centre and the car parking can be tucked away at a lower level allowing the upper levels to be developed in the form of pleasant pedestrian squares and malls.

This method of building across a river valley in order to separate cars from pedestrians was popularised among planning professionals by the unbuilt, but extensively published, plan for a new town at Hook, Hampshire, produced by the London County Council in 1959.

The Dawley plan proceeded in a hesitant and piecemeal fashion, owing not to any uncertainty on Madin's part but seemingly to an initial lack of political confidence. The lack of a motorway connection to Birmingham and the West Midlands is also cited by Madin as an obstacle to early progress. What was novel was his plan for traffic management, for Dawley was the first British new town (with the exception of the unbuilt Hook) to reject a nodal plan for a linear one, with a series of centres linked by a dual carriageway, as advocated by Lewis Mumford in his influential 1938 study *The Culture of Cities*. The draft plan likened the arrangement of housing, shops and schools to 'beads on a necklace', with a southern spur linking the Shropshire town of Madeley to the system. The new housing was to be arranged in small neighbourhoods in groups of eight around the existing towns. At the centre, in Malinslee, was to be a new civic centre and shopping area linked by footpaths to these neighbourhoods and with underground parking. To the south of this was to be a large park. Madin's plans even extended to a site for a university.[4]

While he was drawing up the Dawley plan, Madin had voiced his concern to the Minister for Housing that it excluded the existing settlements of Wellington and Oakengates, north of the A5 (and, later, the M54 motorway), which would thereby lose out on the benefits of being part of a new town. By the end of 1968,

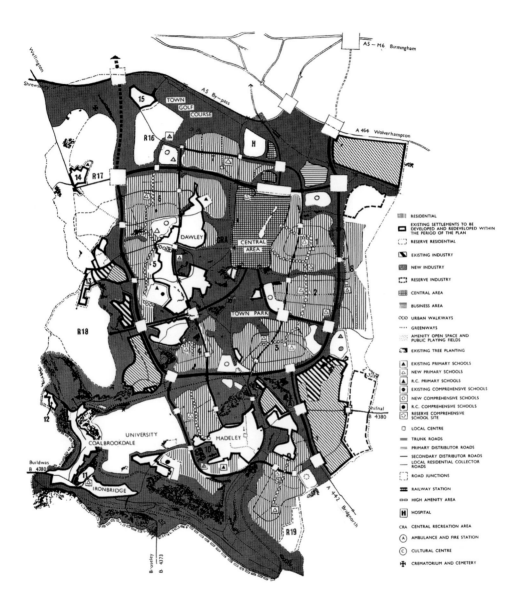

above: The Dawley plan

he had persuaded the minister to extend the area for the new town to encompass Wellington and Oakengates. It then became obvious that this would create a city, which deserved a new name. So, in approving an increase in the population of the new town by 50,000, the minister, by now Arthur Greenwood, renamed it 'Telford' in honour of the great engineer whose Holyhead road passed through the area.

Madin now produced a master plan for the whole Telford area. The dynamic leader of Birmingham City Council, Sir Frank Price, who as Lord Mayor had opened Madin's Hagley House in 1965, was appointed Chairman of Telford Development Corporation. Emrys Thomas from West Bromwich Council became its Chief Executive and stayed until 1980. This new team, comprising men who already knew each other from previous projects, gave the new town the expertise and confidence to progress, although there remained difficulties to overcome. The initial reservations held by Dawley Urban District Council about the development corporation continued throughout its life.[5] However, it would be wrong to ascribe the growing pains of the new town to any lack of skill or foresight in its master planner.

The Telford plan, published in 1969 in two large volumes, was only the first step in a very long process involving generations of planners, architects, housing managers, economic-development staff and estate managers – not to mention the people who would come to live and work in the new town. The report was produced in association with Economic Consultants Limited, the civil engineers Freeman Fox Wilbur Smith & Associates, mining engineers K. Wardell & Partners and the landscape architect J. St Bodfan Gruffydd.[6] The Telford plan was more sophisticated than Madin's earlier plans for Corby and Dawley, and its road network is more prominent than those of earlier examples.

Credit must also be given to Madin and his office for pointing out the archaeological value of the remains of the birthplace of Britain's Industrial Revolution at Ironbridge and Coalbrookdale. In the course of their surveys, they discovered hundreds of abandoned small pit mounds, and adjacent mine shafts where iron and coal had once been mined by hand and pulled out in bags by donkeys or horses. Madin recalls how he came across a cast-iron pig trough that had been in a farmer's field for several generations, and many other artefacts from the beginning of the Industrial Revolution. He gave instructions to the development corporation that these should be stored in a disused quarry until they could be catalogued and properly displayed, and thus began the work that led to the formation of the Ironbridge Gorge Trust and the eventual declaration of the area as a World Heritage Site.

Madin's determination to preserve the best of the past and of the natural landscape can still be seen in the layout of the town, the preserved old cottages and the many reminders of the area's history, such as the wagon wheel that marks the Silkin Way and the tableaux in the modern shopping centre. This approach has given the people

of Telford a lasting legacy, one that softens and humanises the rawness of the new
and modern in the same way that Madin liked to do with his early buildings. Madin's
housing scheme at Brookside (not to be confused with the estate of the same name
in Corby), completed in 1975, was designed around small open spaces, with plenty
of mature trees, in which cars are kept apart from pedestrians. It is well kept today,
although the terrace houses have had new front porches added. The local shopping
centre – also part of the original scheme – is still there, though it is struggling to
survive following changes in retail patterns.

above top: **Cover of the Telford Plan**
above: **Perspective included in the plan illustrating what Telford would be like in 1991**

Unlike a single building, a new town cannot be dismantled or discarded if it does not work. As Madin realised, the plan and its related infrastructure had to serve its purpose for very much longer than the buildings in it. The major elements of the plan are still there today and working as well as, if not better than, most local-authority-owned facilities. The Town Park, which is watched over by an active Friends Group, is a splendid asset, and the traffic-free Silkin Way that runs through the heart of the town is a boon to walkers, runners and cyclists. Madin reflects that 'as built, the villages [the beads on the necklace] were not given enough landscaped space surrounding each village, and the town centre was not built with the planned views over the town park'.[7] Madin's plans for multi-storey parking underneath the shopping centre did not materialise and today it is surrounded by large surface car parks, but the council have recently proposed to build multi-storey facilities that may yet fulfil Madin's original intention.

There was no motorway to Telford in 1965, but by the time the Telford plan was published in 1969, the M54 had been approved for a route cutting east–west just north

above: **Housing at Brookside, Telford, c.1975**

of the new town centre. It brought more industry to Telford from the UK and abroad, although it also made it easier for Telford residents to commute to Wolverhampton or even Birmingham for work.

Notwithstanding subsequently changed attitudes to public housing and services, Telford is today a successful town despite its rather isolated location, inviting comparison with Milton Keynes – the most economically successful of the new towns designated in the late 1960s. It is more difficult to judge the merit of entire new towns and neighbourhoods than single buildings, although it could be argued that the only difference between them is one of scale. It is equally hard to judge how much of a new town's success is due to the skill of its master planner rather than to factors such as location and market economics. At Telford, many more aspects lay beyond the direct control of the master planner than Madin had experienced with the Calthorpe Estate – notably changes in management regimes, as the urban district council gave way to a development corporation, only to revert back to a two-tier local-authority system and now to a unitary council.

Madin himself expressed the enormity and complexity of the task of designing a new town when he said in *Six Men*:

> We are producing an environment in which people are going to live, possibly for another hundred years ... and I think any architect feels that he is really not worthy of creating this environment which is in fact so important to everybody. But all you can do is do the very best you can, at the time, and ensure that you put every possible effort into creating the right environment. But there is a feeling of inadequacy because of the vastness of the problem, particularly in recreating urban areas and designing an environment for people to live in, like a new town for instance.[8]

His new-town master plans may not have been as striking as Arthur Ling's 'figure-of-eight' for Runcorn, Hugh Wilson's 'city-on-a-hill' at Cumbernauld or Richard Llewelyn-Davies's Milton Keynes square grid superimposed on the fields of Buckinghamshire, but they were above all logical and practical.

Back in Birmingham, Madin was asked by the city council in 1965 to prepare a plan for a Comprehensive Development Area on a 15-hectare (37-acre) site off the Pershore Road called Calthorpe Park. Madin's plan contained the mix of low-, medium- and high-rise development of the kind pioneered on the Calthorpe Estate. Four 16-storey blocks were to be located at each end of the estate, 'guarding' the two-storey houses in its centre; between were four-storey maisonette blocks. In the event, no tower blocks were built and by 1975 only 409 dwellings designed by Madin had been constructed: 241 two-storey houses (50 more than intended) and 168 four-storey maisonettes (250 fewer than planned). Since then some piecemeal development has taken place, but a number of plots still remain vacant.

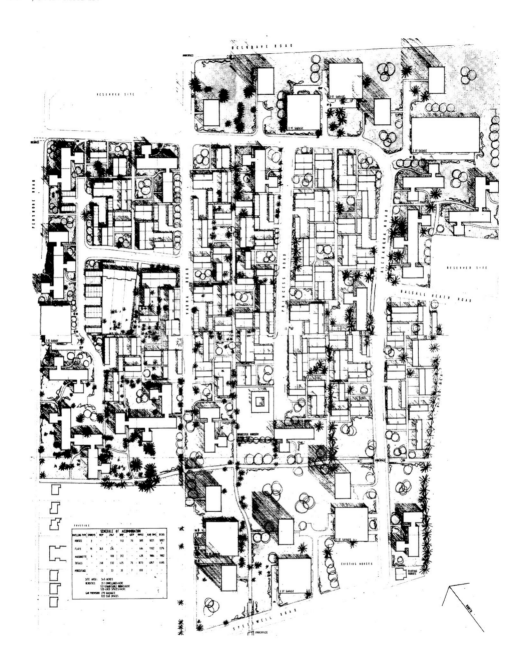

above: Plan of the Calthorpe Park Comprehensive Development Area

The 1970s was a time of growth for voluntary housing associations, to which Madin made a contribution. At Maney Hill, close to the centre of Sutton Coldfield, he built an estate of three-storey flats for the Second Bromford Housing Society Limited. Madin took his usual care to respect the existing landscape, around which the uncompromisingly modernist housing blocks were carefully arranged. They are now managed by an agent in Tamworth and are still looking good and well cared for.

Not far from the Calthorpe Estate and close to his parents' house in Moseley, on land at Belle Walk, Bromford Warden Housing Association appointed Madin to plan and

above: Co-ownership housing, Wake Green Park Phase 2, mid-1970s

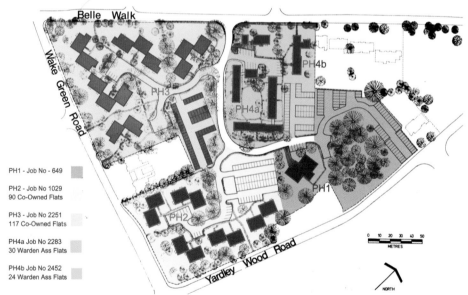

PH1 - Job No - 649

PH2 - Job No 1029
90 Co-Owned Flats

PH3 - Job No 2251
117 Co-Owned Flats

PH4a Job No 2283
30 Warden Ass Flats

PH4b Job No 2452
24 Warden Ass Flats

Wake Green Park - Moseley - Bromford Housing Association

above top: Warden-assisted apartments, Wake Green Park Phase 4a – photograph taken in the mid-1970s
above: Overall plan and key of Wake Green Park

design a block of 30 elderly persons' dwellings together with warden's accommodation and communal facilities. On the same site, Bromford Park, 249 two- and three-person flats and bedsitters with garages for the Bromford Housing Association were constructed in phases between 1967 and 1974. These schemes have since been incorporated into a gated community called Wake Green Park, which is managed commercially by MetroPM.

The concept of new towns as receptacles for overspill population from large cities like Birmingham lasted only until the mid-1970s, when economic recession and the rise of the conservation movement forced more investment into inner-city regeneration. However, faced with a sudden rise in population after many fairly static years, the government has lately proposed a number of 'eco-towns' in the countryside, the designers of which could benefit from the experience of Madin's generation of new-town planners.

Notes

1. In David Chapman (ed.), *Region and Renaissance 1950 to 2000*, 2000, pp48–9.

2. Hilary Millward, *Window on Edgbaston*, 1962.

3. René Cutforth, *Six Men*.

4. Nikolaus Pevsner, *The Buildings of England, Shropshire*, 1966, pp619–25; revised by John Newman for Yale University Press, 2006, pp619–24.

5. Maurice de Soissons, *Telford, the Making of Shropshire's New Town*, 1991, p528.

6. John Madin Design Group, *Telford Development Proposals*, Volume 1, 1969.

7. Letter from John Madin to the author, 22 March 2010.

8. Cutforth, *op. cit.*

5   Building for leisure

The collection of pioneering leisure developments that Madin was commissioned to design may have owed something to his own love of outdoor activity. He was a keen skier, but had a particular love of water sports and sailing. He was filmed water-skiing and dinghy sailing on Edgbaston's Rotton Park Reservoir in *Six Men*, and he later owned a Mediterranean-based ocean-going yacht.[1] Born in a city that is further from the sea than any other in the United Kingdom, he now lives on the banks of the River Hamble near Southampton.

Many commentators in the 1960s predicted that people in developed societies would have much more leisure time as computers and robots freed them from the drudgery of long working hours. It was also widely expected that increasing personal wealth would lead to an expanding market for holiday homes, both in the UK and abroad, while cheaper fares would open up more foreign holiday resorts. The inaccuracy of some of these predictions, and the mixed fortunes of the many leisure projects in which Madin was involved, illustrate how vulnerable the sector has been to changes in economic and political fortunes, individually and on an international scale.

Madin's philosophy of playing as hard as he worked led to an early commission from Shirley Golf Club, which had been founded in 1955 on the edge of the conurbation in Solihull. Madin was asked to design the clubhouse – a single-storey building with a lounge, bar, committee room and changing rooms. It was opened in July 1959 and is still in use and in good order.

The design incorporated a prominent external chimney, built in rough stone, which contrasts strikingly with a butterfly roof and large windows. The chimney suggests the influence of Frank Lloyd Wright and the butterfly roof that of Le Corbusier and Marcel Breuer on Madin's generation, and these elements humanise what might have been a clinical, machine-made look.

Free time for people in the Birmingham area was extensively catered for by the large brewers – notably Mitchells and Butler of Cape Hill, who commissioned a series of small new pubs from Madin. The Covered Wagon, opened in 1962 in Yardley Wood Road, is a typical example that is still recognisably his design despite many recent alterations to the windows.

Madin's St Martin's Youth Centre in Gooch Street, Birmingham, was opened by Princess Alexandra in 1968. It was a purpose-built youth centre for the Anglican Church in a redevelopment area, and included an open play area at first-floor roof level. It is still very much in use today, although showing signs of wear from the heavy use experienced by such facilities.

opposite: Wardija Hill Top Village, Malta, 2010

above top: Madin water-skiing on Edgbaston Reservoir 1965
above: Shirley Golf Club, 1959

Bron-y-Mor

The first large-scale opportunity for Madin to provide for the growing demand for holiday homes by the sea came when in 1961 he was asked to plan a seaside village for 3,000 people on a 16-hectare (40-acre) site between the Cambrian Coast railway and the sea near Tywyn at Bron-y-Mor (Sea Brink in translation). The west coast of Wales has long been a seaside destination for Midlanders – particularly those from Birmingham – with its good train service to Aberystwyth, Aberdyfi, Barmouth and Pwllheli, where Billy Butlin opened one of his holiday camps in 1947. The Outward Bound School, where Madin sailed with his young family, was based in Aberdyfi.

The *Architects' Journal* described Bron-y-Mor as a new seaside resort for Wales.[2] The brief was to provide 769 dwellings and a 12-storey hotel, with an entertainment centre and a lido with a sliding roof, for which Madin supplied sketches and a model. The design was based on the complete segregation of pedestrians and vehicles. The architect Clough Williams-Ellis, whose Portmeirion village had been taking shape up the coast on the Mawddach Estuary since 1925, was said to have admired the original layout, with its small courtyards. Madin proposed a brave plan, with the hotel at right angles to the seafront.[3] It was never fully implemented owing, in Madin's view, to the subsequent economic recession, but two blocks of balconied flats in Llewelyn Street (Ty Meirion and Ty Ceredig) were built, as were a row of bungalows with steep-pitched roofs. A

above: **Architect's perspective of the seafront hotel, Bron-y-Mor**

large field at the centre of the site has been given over to two tall radio masts and other plots remain undeveloped, giving the scheme a half-completed appearance and, without the planned courtyards, leaving it exposed to the westerly sea breezes. Although this pioneering planned seaside village was not completed according to Madin's master plan, the realised flats and bungalows were given a Ministry of Housing and Local Government Housing Award in 1964.

Holiday villages abroad

Madin's knowledge of boats and sailing, as well as his town-planning and housing skills, was put to good use in designing marina villages around the British and Mediterranean coasts. Some of the developments were quite urban, and borrowed elements from his commercial modern architectural vocabulary, while others were freer in their layout. He produced a 'light' architecture, which both created a holiday atmosphere and respected the vernacular character of local buildings, especially those around the Mediterranean.

At L'Erée, on the west coast of Guernsey, Madin drew up a detailed development plan in 1963 for a 16-hectare (40-acre) residential and holiday community, including a hotel, shopping and social centre, holiday apartments and permanent residences.

It was the then chairman of Dawley Development Corporation, Sir Reginald Pearson, who introduced Madin to Borg Olivier, at that time the Prime Minister and Minister of Economic Planning and Finance in the Maltese Government, who needed advice on how to exploit the island's tourist potential. Growing numbers of wealthy people from the UK and mainland Europe were buying property in Malta not only because of its climate, fine coastline and rugged limestone scenery, but because income tax was levied on new residents at only five pence in the pound. As a result, house prices had risen tenfold in five years and there was a rush to build new dwellings or renovate existing ones. Olivier introduced Madin to the owner of a number of hilltop sites on the island, the first of which overlooked the port of Wardija. The plan for the Wardija Hill Top Village, the first phase of which was completed in 1972, comprised 200 units, a hotel and associated facilities. Other schemes were designed at El Madliena and Golden Sands. Madin used limestone cut out of the hillside by the experienced local stone-masons, with whom he enjoyed working.

At Malta's General Election in 1971, the Nationalist Olivier was defeated by the Labour party under Dom Mintoff, who abolished the tax advantages for foreigners and brought the property development boom to a halt. The later phases of Wardija Hill Top Village were left uncompleted.[4]

Madin's familiarity with Cairo from his army days may have helped him to win a commission in 1966 from the Egyptian Government to prepare a plan for Nile City, a new development on the banks of the River Nile, the traditional tourist route between Cairo and the temples of southern Egypt. Another commission followed, to plan the redevelopment of part of western Cairo.

On the island of Cyprus the peace between the Turkish and Greek communities had to be enforced by the United Nations in 1964, but there was for a while a tourist development policy like that on Malta. When giving a lecture on planning at an international symposium in Cairo, Madin met the Cypriot Minister of Finance, Renos Solomides, who introduced him to President Makarios. Between 1968 and 1974 Madin drew up plans for new tourist villages at Lara, on Peace Hill overlooking Kyrenia, and

above top: First phase of Wardija Hill Top Village, Malta, 1979
above: Architect's model, Wardija Hill Top Village

on a historic hilltop called Campbell Battery. The first phase of Peace Hill, built using the local traditional method of white-painted stucco walls and red-tiled roofs, was close to completion when Turkey invaded northern Cyprus in 1974, halting any further development.

Libya became very international in its outlook in the 1960s, and in 1968 its Minister of Tourism sought Madin's advice about a new seaside resort in the Mellaha Road district of Tripoli, a new television centre and a house for his own use. The design of these projects was well advanced in 1969 when Colonel Gaddafi came to power and instituted an era of hostility to the West.

The French Government was meanwhile promoting the development of marina villages on the Mediterranean coast, the most famous of which was the Venetian-style

above top: Model of hilltop village, Peace Hill, Kyrenia, Cyprus
above: Architect's perspective of coastal development, Mellaha Highway, Tripoli, Libya

Port Grimaud designed by François Spoerry. Madin was commissioned in 1973 to plan a village at Port d'Hyères, on the coast just east of Toulon, based around a new 1,000-berth marina and 800 dwellings. He completed the plan in 1975.

At Mays Landing in Hamilton Township, New Jersey, Madin prepared a master plan between 1980 and 1989 for 300 houses and apartments within a golf course and business park.

Madin's final overseas project was the design of the Biniorella Hilltop Village and marina on the south coast of Mallorca between the ports of Puerto Portals and Andraix. The proposals were granted preliminary approval in 1992, just before it was announced by the Madrid Government that no more new marinas would be allowed.

Madin's abiding passion for sailing and his interest in the design of land-based sailing facilities is revealed in a paper of 1994, in which he concisely reviewed the previous 30 years of marina development in Europe and the USA.[5] He questioned why national and local governments thought that the new 'parks for boats' could be planned separately from the adjacent land area, and why they imagined that they would have little or no impact on the surrounding region. He believed that the authorities in question had not considered these matters and the result, he wrote, 'is to be seen before our very eyes in the devastation that has been wrought to many thousands of miles of natural coastline of the Mediterranean. Devastation which has been wrought by over zealous development and the profit motive principally to satisfy the package holiday market'. Instead, he offered his own vision of a marina in which, as he put it:

> the sea defence walls are built of the local natural stone and are not
> designed in rigid straight lines but are sensitively curved reflecting the

above: **Housing and marina, Port d'Hyères, France**

above top: The Royal Southern Yacht Club from the River Hamble, 2010
above: The Royal Southern Yacht Club, interior, 2010

natural landscape. The buildings on the water front, the restaurants, cafes,
bars and hotels are no more than two or three storeys high reflecting the
human scale and in harmony with the size of most yachts in the marinas.
They are built in natural materials and the design reflects the older tradi-
tional buildings of the area.

Close to his home on the banks of the Hamble, near Southampton, is the Royal
Southern Yacht Club. When Madin joined it in 1992 it consisted of a collection of listed
houses with piecemeal extensions. He prepared a comprehensive long-term plan for the
club that could be implemented in phases as funds became available. Later, he joined
the committee and designed the new club house – including the interior, the furniture
and carpets incorporating the motif of the Club flag – as a gift. It was opened by the
Duke of Edinburgh in 1998.[6]

Aberdyfi

Madin's attachment to the west coast of Wales dates back to 1961 when he asked a friend
who owned a light aircraft to fly him along the whole of the Welsh coast in order to pick
out a village where he could make a holiday home for his family. He chose the ancient
seaport village of Aberdyfi (in English, 'Aberdovey'), where he bought a Victorian
terrace house on the front in 1962–3 and converted it into two apartments. In the
summer of 1966, Madin learned that a local farmer was about to sell a large field above
the village to a private property developer, so he quickly stepped in and bought the land
to prevent it being built over in a piecemeal and unsatisfactory manner. Madin recalls
that the chairman of the planning committee, who lived in Aberdyfi, congratulated him
on stopping the development and, knowing his work at Telford, invited him to draw
up a plan for the site – in effect a master plan for the extension of the village. Madin
produced a proposal for 400 houses and apartments of various types in a landscaped
setting on the hillside, which was welcomed by the committee. A planning application
was approved by Merioneth County Council in 1967. Madin recalls feeling that a great
responsibility had been placed on his shoulders, to maintain the character of Aberdyfi
while providing houses and apartments for those who wanted to enjoy its wonderful
unspoilt environment. He believes that the carefully controlled slow pace of development within the agreed master plan has served to reassure the people of Aberdyfi
that his original objective is being fulfilled.

In the lower part of the site Madin has created a self-catering holiday village,
Aberdovey Hillside Village. This comprises houses and flats in pairs or short terraces,
following the contours of the land, pebble-dashed and with balconies. The first pair,
Eastward and Westward, were built in 1967 with a split-level interior and split roof – the
former for Madin's family and members of staff to use. The more exposed upper site was
developed with rendered houses cut into the slope.[7]

The Hillside Village now comprises 20 apartments and houses that accommodate
some 3,000 visitors every year, some of whom are 'regulars', who bring significant

trade to local businesses. It is a self-catering holiday village company administered by professional staff, with a well-equipped children's playroom and a games room on the small square opposite the office. The roads are un-metalled and unadopted by the local authority, and lighting is by small lamps at the side of the footpaths. A slate-paved public footpath winds up the hill along the western boundary wall of the site and through the upper part of the open and as yet undeveloped site. Another footpath runs just outside the southern boundary. At first sight it reminds one of Portmeirion, on a similar site on the Mawddach Estuary – especially the original apartments and houses on the lowest part of the site, with their pebble-dashed walls and brown woodwork, which are set among the blue-grey slate retaining walls and boundary walls.

Madin is still actively involved in completing Hillside Park, designing houses and apartments in a landscaped setting in accordance with the original master plan. The development is proceeding slowly, as was originally intended. In order to ensure that the landscaping and buildings here are maintained to the highest standard, Madin has formed a not-for-profit maintenance company.[8]

The highly controlled approach to property development by which Madin manages gradual change within an overall framework is consistent with his long-held values,

above: **Aberdovey Hillside Village, 2010**

but he has not always been in a position to implement his ideas to the full as he can at Aberdyfi. He believes that he can create a modern architectural legacy here that also respects the natural features of the location, as he did with such success in the leafy suburb of Edgbaston at the start of his career. He has also put in place the legal framework to protect that legacy from unsympathetic change in the future.

Notes

1. René Cutforth, *Six Men*, 1962.
2. *Architects' Journal*, 26 July 1961, p110.
3. Richard Haslam, Julian Orbach and Adam Voelcker, *The Buildings of Wales*, Gwynedd, 2009, p18, includes a drawing by Madin of this scheme.
4. Images can be seen at www.wardijahilltopvillage.com
5. John Madin, 'Design and Development of Marinas and Environmental Considerations', unpublished paper, c.1994.
6. 'Royal Southern Yacht Club', *Southern*, vol. 5 no. 3, August 1998. A special edition of the newsletter, with photographs of the recently completed building and John and Judy Madin with the Commodore.
7. Haslam, Orbach and Voelcker, *op. cit.*, p538.
8. The website address for the Aberdovey Hillside Village is www.hillsidevillage.co.uk

6 Civic pride

The relationship between official architects and those in private practice plays an important part in the story of civic architecture and planning in Birmingham. Madin worked with four City Architects over a period of some 20 years. Cities have periodically employed consultant architects to draw up grand plans and to design their major civic buildings. However, in the 20th century most additionally appointed a salaried City Architect, whose department evolved out of that of an older institution, the City Engineer and Surveyor. In Birmingham this process occurred relatively late, when A. G. Sheppard Fidler was appointed City Architect in 1952. Herbert Manzoni had previously combined the roles of engineer, architect and town planner, and although he had been the young Madin's mentor in the war, the two later disagreed how the city centre should be replanned. Manzoni had a reputation for caring little about the past, and he believed that modern buildings should have a lifespan of no more than 15 or 20 years.[1]

Madin developed a very good working relationship with Sheppard Fidler and his successor from 1964 , J. R. Sherridan Shedden (until Shedden's sudden death in 1966). He was replaced by Alan Maudsley, who was City Architect when Madin was working on the Central Library but whose subsequent conviction for corruption brought the office into disrepute.

Civic Centre plans

Since the 1920s, Birmingham's leaders had dreamed of a new civic centre worthy of England's second city. A succession of grand plans was drawn up, covering a large area from the Council House and Town Hall along both sides of Broad Street to the old Bingley Hall. The corporation organised an open competition for the layout of this area in 1926, but the winning scheme, by Maximilian Romanoff of Paris, proved too expensive. A second project was approved in 1934, comprising two large blocks of administrative offices, a natural history museum, a City Hall and a public library. Another competition was held the next year, open only to British architects, which was won by T. Cecil Howitt of Nottingham. Building began in 1938 but only one range of council offices, Baskerville House, was completed before the outbreak of war. Madin advised the City Planners on the need for a three-dimensional master plan for the city centre, but his advice was not then heeded. It was only as the financial situation eased in the late 1950s that the civic centre scheme was reconsidered, and Sheppard Fidler presented a master plan for the area in 1960 as a pedestrian precinct linked to the older

opposite: The entrance hall of Birmingham Central Library soon after it was opened

civic buildings in Victoria and Chamberlain squares. However, by the time that Pevsner and Wedgwood toured Birmingham in the early 1960s this plan had already become obsolete.[2]

Madin's proposals

Madin was asked in 1964 by Sherridan Shedden to collaborate on a new civic-centre master plan, incorporating an ensemble of buildings at the eastern end of Broad Street on the site known as Paradise Circus. This 'rump' of Sheppard Fidler's scheme reflected the city's more realistic but nevertheless impressive ambitions. Madin produced a large model, exhibited in April 1965, showing the Town Hall of 1832–4 and the Hall of Memory war memorial, a Portland stone classical domed octagon from 1922–5, together with a bus station, student halls of residence, a concert hall, library, blocks of flats, a new monorail terminal, a 140-metre (460-foot) restaurant tower with a viewing platform, a repertory theatre, exhibition hall, planetarium, offices and car parks. Madin was responsible for the design of the Paradise Circus site, and James A. Roberts for the exhibition hall on the south-east side of Broad Street. The idea was to link the Council House (1874–85) with Baskerville House through a series of pedestrian court-

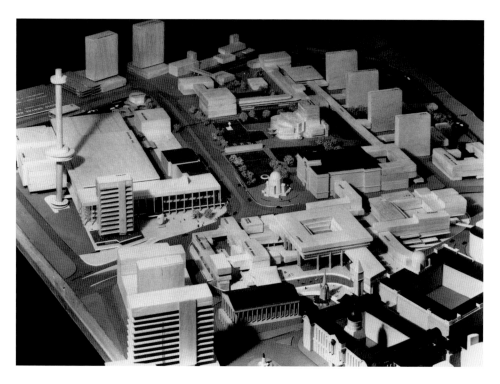

above: **The Civic Centre model**

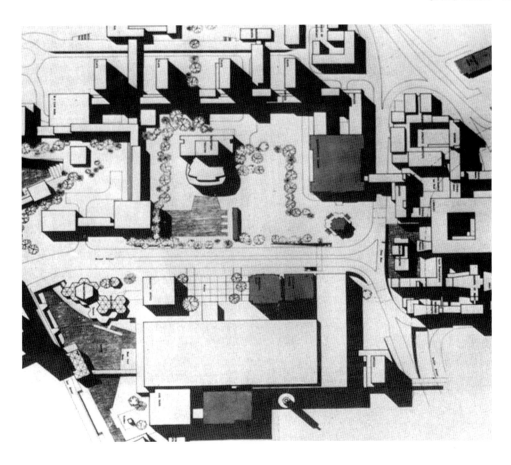

yards decorated with fountains, pools and waterfalls, and surrounded by a collection
of major buildings that would meet the cultural, educational and recreational needs of
Birmingham people. The accompanying press statement declared that:

> *Complete segregation of pedestrians from traffic has been achieved in this
> plan for Birmingham's Civic Centre. People will be able to walk unhin-
> dered through a series of linked squares, precincts and courts, or to sit and
> admire the fine views carefully contrived by making the most of a variety of
> levels. A special attraction in the scheme will be at least six water gardens,
> including the landscaping of two old canal basins. There are two main
> levels throughout the site. Cars, buses and lorries will circulate on the lower
> level and entries have been kept to a minimum. Above this will be the main
> pedestrian level at which the squares and courts are sited. The buildings are
> to be grouped into 'use zones' around these precincts, creating quiet areas.*

above: **The Civic Centre plan**

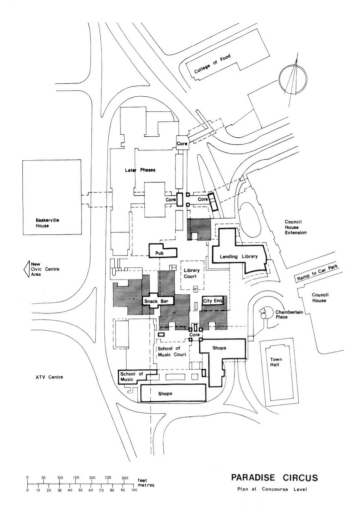

PARADISE CIRCUS

Plan at Concourse Level

Madin's plan for Paradise Circus was approved by the council in 1968. The site was a complicated one, encircled and tunnelled under by new roads. The original scheme was for a central library, with a bus station underneath, a school of music and a physical sports institute. With so many public buildings, this was to be for Madin the 'civic heart' of the city. The new Central Library was to be its centrepiece, and was carefully placed in Chamberlain Square to relate to the historic Town Hall and Council House.

Reflecting the concerns of the time – and particularly Colin Buchanan's report of 1963, *Traffic in Towns* – Madin separated pedestrians from vehicles by designing the library on a platform and linking it to the Council House and Baskerville House with

above: The Paradise Circus plan

high-level pedestrian bridges.[3] These bridges were never built and only the intended exit point of one can still be seen, on the façade of the Reference Library facing Centenary Square. The council's proposal that the library should have its own bus station beneath it was a radical concept for a city so wedded to the car, even at a time when the buses were owned and run by Birmingham Corporation itself.

The Central Library

Birmingham's first central library was built west of the Town Hall in 1864–5 and designed by William Martin and John Henry Chamberlain in the classical style. When it was gutted by fire in 1879, it was rebuilt in a boisterous Italianate idiom by Chamberlain and reopened in 1882. By 1938, the city council had decided that a new library was 'an urgent necessity', but nothing was done about it until 1956, when the City Librarian, Victor Woods, was asked to report. The official and often-repeated explanation that the old library stood in the way of the proposed ring road is an oversimplification. It was not on the direct line of the road, which in any case goes through a tunnel well underneath the new library, but reflects the need shared by many cities for bigger and more wide-ranging reference collections, as well as Birmingham's enduring passion for sweeping away its recent past to make way for the latest fashion. There are still many who mourn the loss of Chamberlain's library and others who question the use of the label 'not fit for the next century' to justify both its destruction and the proposal to destroy its replacement.

above: **Model of Paradise Circus**

A site for the new library was selected next to the old one in 1959, and in 1960 a general specification was agreed. In 1963 a box-like proposal by the City Architect was rejected by the council, and in 1964 Madin was commissioned to carry out a new design. At the same time, William Arthur Taylor was appointed City Librarian in part for his particular interest in new libraries, having already been involved in the design of one for the Nigerian Government. One of Taylor's most important additions to the brief was that there should be a Children's Library, with its own entrance and a workshop area for painting, puppetry and other activities. No children's library was included in the first brief since relatively few youngsters lived nearby, but Taylor argued that it was precisely the inner-city schools which were most old-fashioned and in need of good external facilities. Even today, the Central Library draws most of its users from the Ladywood ward in which it stands. Just as innovative was Taylor's decision to include Commercial and Quick Reference libraries – the latter an informal readers' lounge within the Lending Library. Madin began work by visiting several new libraries in the USA, where he learned much about the likely effect of digital technology on library services.

By July 1965, the new library project had taken precedence over the rest of the civic-centre redevelopment. The design in its final form was published in July 1966 and

above: Architect's perspective of the School of Music Court Central Library, Paradise Circus

encompassed far more functions than a standard library – including administrative offices serving the city's 35 branch libraries, meeting rooms, book-processing and binding facilities, and loading bays. It housed for the first time within a single building all the library's varied collections, including the municipal archives. The reference collection, and in particular the Business Library, was very large and the Shakespeare Memorial Library – founded in 1864 – was a growing antiquarian collection of international importance. Construction began in 1969 and the main shell was completed in 1971. The structural engineer was Ove Arup & Partners, and the main contractor was Sir Robert McAlpine and Sons. Fitting-out took until 1973. The formal opening by future Prime Minister Harold Wilson was on 12 January 1974, at which point it was said to be the largest municipal library in Europe.

The library's outward form is simple and comprises the massive reference block and the smaller lending block to its east, which also houses the first set of escalators leading to the upper floors of both libraries. The eight-storey, square reference block was designed around an open lightwell or 'atrium' above a public square that could be entered from all four sides by walking beneath the building itself, which was raised above the sloping ground level by two or three storeys. The square was to be enhanced by a series of ornamental pools, and around it were intended to be a pub, a snack bar and a city information office. Of these only the pub, The Yardbird, was built as Madin intended, attached to the west side of the reference block.

Above these float the cantilevered floors of the library, each larger than the one below resulting in the distinctive inverted ziggurat formation. This was a popular motif in the 1960s, derived ultimately from Sant'Elia's drawings for 'Casa a gradinate', and Marcel Breuer's 1928 scheme for a hospital at Elberfeld, which had a stepped section. It was adopted for civic purposes in the monumental Boston City Hall by Kallmann, McKinnell and Knowles, won in competition in 1962. John Ericsson, a member of Madin's design team for the library, says that he became aware of the Boston City Hall design only later; in conversation with Andy Foster he gave the principal source for Birmingham City Library as Leslie Martin's library complex at St Cross, Oxford, coupled with an admiration for Denys Lasdun's Royal College of Physicians and Le Corbusier's monastery of La Tourette.[4] On the outside the windows are restricted to narrow high-level strips, but the central atrium is completely glazed behind deep concrete balconies. This introverted arrangement suited the Reference Library, making it exceptionally conducive to study; although there is good natural light where most needed, the design was an early recognition of the problems of solar gain and the damage that the sun can do to books. The structure is supported on a square of 12 reinforced-concrete columns with spans of ten metres (32 feet) over the bus interchange and loading bays below. Externally they appear as four huge vertical punctuations on each façade, which rise into and support the strong horizontals of the cantilevered library floors.

The much smaller lending block, with its welcoming three-storey façade, was designed to house the main entrance, the Lending Library and the Children's Library.

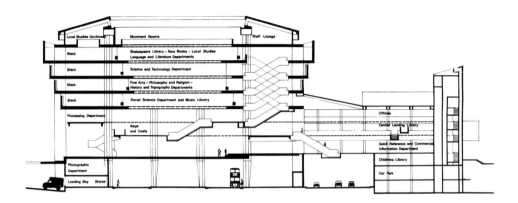

This façade has a slight curve facing Chamberlain Square, which contrasts well with the rectangular geometry of the main block. The double-height main entrance hall between the lending and reference blocks is entirely glazed on the side facing the atrium, and is an early example of a freestanding wall made of toughened glass of the kind later made famous by Norman Foster with his offices for Willis Faber Dumas in Ipswich (1972–5). Before it was blocked by later shop units in Paradise Forum, the glazed wall allowed the main entrance to be flooded with natural light as well as affording library users a glimpse of the Town Hall and Council House as they rode up and down the escalators.

For the cladding of the buildings, Madin offered the council a choice of Portland stone or travertine marble, out of respect for the adjacent white stone buildings and because he had deployed these materials very successfully before. The building could not have been condemned as a 'concrete monstrosity' had his proposals been accepted. However, a third and cheaper option was that of pre-cast concrete with a stone aggregate, offered by Maudsley and accepted by the council for the main façades as an economic measure. Much of the concrete incorporates a Hopton Wood aggregate that gives it greater warmth than Portland stone. Nonetheless, it was the failure of some of the concrete panels that was cited by the council in 1999 as a reason to demolish the library and pass the site to a commercial developer.

The concrete cast on site, however, is of an exceptionally high quality and finish. The bush-hammered columns and the coffered ceilings of bare smooth concrete straight from their steel moulds give unity and restfulness to the interior. Perhaps Madin foresaw the coming cuts in budgets when he stipulated that the interior should need no maintenance. Unfortunately the building's managers have responded to user complaints about the lack of light – caused by the enclosure of the atrium – by painting some of

above: **Section through Reference Library with bus station**

above top: Central Library from Chamberlain Square, mid-1980s
above: Central Library from Chamberlain Square, 2010

the ceilings white. Not only does this remove direct visual contact with the structural concrete, thus destroying the interior's Brutalist purity, but it commits the management to frequent repainting instead of a once-in-a-lifetime 'wash-and-brush-up'. Elsewhere, the management has painted over the concrete walls also, apparently thinking that they were cheering the place up.

The main Reference Library – including the Shakespeare Library of antiquarian books and manuscripts – was arranged under nine subject headings on the four upper floors. The Record Library, then still a relatively new feature in public libraries, was also here, along with the administrative and service functions, while the archives occupied the top floor. The library aimed to provide 'open access' to all its books, which numbered over 900,000 volumes. As no basement was possible because of the low-level roads, and a tall bookstack was thought inappropriate because of the surrounding buildings, storage is on the same level as the corresponding reading areas, making for ready access and easy flexibility should

above: **The Science & Technology Department of the Reference Library, c.1975**

more space be required for one or the other. The dual purpose of each floor led to the relatively low ceiling height of three metres (ten feet) required for stacks; by opening up wells in the ceilings of some of the public areas, more expansive double-height spaces provide relief and interest. Taylor wanted all the departments to be linked, so that a user of one section of the library would be aware of the rest, and this resulted in the complex glazed entrance and the escalator system that runs through the heart of the building.

Adjacent to the Central Library in Paradise Circus is Birmingham's best-kept secret, not easily appreciated from the outside: the Birmingham School of Music, or Conservatoire, opened in 1973. It consists of a suite of rehearsal studios, performance rooms and a medium-sized concert hall, the Adrian Boult Hall (opened in 1983), as well as all the accommodation needed for the academic staff of this department of Birmingham City University. The exterior architecture of the Conservatoire is unremarkable, but inside one finds all the facilities and auditoria needed by a lively and exciting school of music set in the heart of the city close to Birmingham Symphony Hall, the restored Town Hall and the fine music department of the Central Library. The 520-seat Adrian Boult Hall brings the music-loving public into the school for student concerts, and provides a worthy medium-sized venue for local amateur and professional choirs and orchestras.

above: **Architect's perspective of the Central Library from the west**

Also completed in 1986, although based on a scheme by Madin from 1969–70, is the 200-seat Library Theatre attached to the west side of the reference block, and always intended to be shared by the library and the School of Music. The result of a design-and-build commission awarded to Henry Boot Projects, it was regarded by Andy Foster as 'timid' compared to the Central Library itself.[5] Madin did not approve of design-and-build as a procurement method, and personally had no involvement in the theatre as realised. Nevertheless, as set at the corner of one of the main façades, and with its curvaceous form clad in narrow vertical pre-cast concrete panels above a glazed ground floor, the Library Theatre forms the perfect foil to the horizontals of the Reference Library that towers over and above it. Just inside the concourse-level entrance to the Library Theatre is the Shakespeare Memorial Room, which was reconstructed from the former Reference Library. It is a jewel-like fragment of the Victorian glory of the old library, a token memento of a well-loved building and suggests that the city fathers felt some regret at its loss. The cast-iron spiral staircase removed from the old building and now connecting the top floors of the Central Library performs a similar symbolic role, like a lock of hair from a dead friend.

The last of Madin's Civic Trust awards was given for his sensitive restoration of the Victorian Chamberlain Memorial and the remodelling of the public space in front of his Central Library. Here, Madin made the best possible use of the slope in the ground from the steps of Birmingham Museum and Art Gallery and the town hall to the concourse underneath the Central Library ziggurat by designing a semicircular amphitheatre to enclose the fountain. The amphitheatre is not only practical but has become a very popular place for medium-scale public events and seasonal celebrations, such as the summertime 'beach' and Santa's Christmas grotto. The proposed new amphitheatre in Centenary Square is a flattering imitation of what is a very successful piece of urban design.

The failure of the city council to fully implement even the relatively modest original plan for Paradise Circus remains a great disappointment to Madin, and demonstrates an inability common among councils in the 1960s to see approved plans through to completion. Madin planned that the land to the north of the library should be used for a physical sports institute, but the severe public spending cuts of the 1970s and the council's decision to sell off parcels of its land to private developers killed the dream of a publicly financed, owned and managed civic centre occupying the entire Paradise Circus site.

Other civic work

Madin was invited by the city council in 1970 to make a detailed study for a new concert hall for the City of Birmingham Symphony Orchestra (CBSO) within the wider civic centre. He produced a preliminary design, an artist's impression and a flow diagram, but was not asked to take it any further. This seems to have been owing to the difficulty of raising the necessary public finance amid the subsequent economic downturn. When Simon Rattle arrived as conductor in 1980, pressure began to grow for a purpose-built concert hall with double the capacity of the old Town Hall. A delegation of city councillors was persuaded during a visit to Chicago and Cleveland, Ohio, that Birmingham's future lay in business tourism, and the idea of the International Convention Centre and Symphony Hall was born. By then, Madin had retired from JMDG and the job went to the Percy Thomas Partnership with Renton Howard Wood Levin. The new hall finally opened in 1991 at the western end of what was to become Centenary Square, 21 years after Madin produced his feasibility study. The remaining elements of the council's wider plans for the civic centre proceeded in a piecemeal fashion or not at all. The council wanted a new exhibition centre in the city centre, but instead the National Exhibition Centre was built on a greenfield site to the east of the city in 1975.

During the long gestation period of the Central Library, Madin was commissioned by the council to design an extension to the Alexandra Theatre, already rebuilt in 1935 by Roland Satchwell. The theatre was acquired by Birmingham Corporation from its private owners in 1969 and sublet to a board of directors, several of whom were city councillors – thus making it, in effect, a municipal enterprise. The site is constricted, and when the inner ring road was built the opportunity was taken to add a new foyer and entrance to the theatre, bridging the street, in a dignified modern style similar to that adopted by Madin for his bank buildings around this time.

above: **Redditch Central Library**

Madin's reputation as a library designer led to a commission for a library in the new town of Redditch, in a scheme first promoted by its urban district council and developed by the new Hereford and Worcester County Council following government reorganisation. It opened in 1976. Although not on the same scale as the Birmingham library, and with a brick facing rather than concrete, there are similarities in the strongly modelled design with its coffered ceilings and overhangs that form a covered way to the street. Inside there is a ramp, rather than escalators, which gives surprise views across the interesting internal spaces and out into the town. The library offered a complete range of facilities to serve the new town population of 90,000 and also surrounding districts.[6]

Changes to Paradise Circus

In 1989, the Birmingham City Architect's Department drew up proposals to glaze in the central atrium of the Central Library. The text accompanying the artist's impression on its publication read: 'Outside the Central Library complex it can be bleak and windy. A new initiative, known as Paradise Forum, will change all that. It will create an outdoors-style eating and entertainment area within the central court under the Central Library, which will be roofed over and enclosed in glass'.[7] Sadly the seductive perspective that gave the impression of a leafy indoor Continental-style street scene did not translate into reality. The space was effectively privatised when it was leased to a property company who sublet securable units for shops, fast-food outlets and restaurants. The part of the basement designed as a bus station has since been used by the library to store archive material, while other elements have become service yards for the tenants of Paradise Forum.

The council decided in 1999 that the whole of Paradise Circus should be sold to a private developer. At first the council felt it unnecessary to justify the idea, but it then became part of its concept of repositioning Birmingham as a desirable centre for inter-national business. Many interdependent elements had to be resolved to ensure the success of the whole project. These included relocating the Central Library and School of Music, reassembling its landholdings in the site by buying back the interests it had dispersed, promoting the area as a world-class business location, funding a new library and clearing the site amid the constraints of the ring road below. Nonetheless, the new Conservative and Liberal Democrat council elected in 2004 continued to support the policy. It resolved in 2007 that the new library should go to Centenary Square on the car park between Baskerville House and the Repertory Theatre, a site rejected as too small in 1999.

A fresh appreciation of the Central Library began to emerge after the council had declared its intention to demolish it. The movement was led by artists and writers who were intrigued by its abstract three-dimensional quality and who were mainly of the generation born in the 1960s or early 1970s that had grown up with the library. Katherina Grosse (b.1961) used it as a canvas for her spray-paintwork in 2002. The effect

was to draw attention to, and visually dissolve, the hard angular structure with bright yellow, green, red and orange paint. Architectural conservationists moved to defend the library in 2003 when the Twentieth Century Society applied to have it statutorily listed. This attempt failed because the government rejected English Heritage's firm recommendation that the library fully merited listed status. In 2006, a small photographic exhibition, 'Back to the Modern', celebrated the library's history and architecture using a mixture of archive and contemporary photographs.[8] One commentator wrote in the visitors' book that 'it brings back to the front the truth of the much distorted perception of Modernism and beauty. It is a concept reflecting the era and its influence on the best of contemporary architecture'. At the same time, artist Perry Roberts (b.1954) was

above: City Council's proposals for Paradise Forum

inspired by the Central Library and other modern buildings in Birmingham to produce a series of wall-sized, slow-moving videos entitled 'Transition'. This ran for two months at the Ikon Gallery, whose director, Jonathan Watkins, wrote in the accompanying catalogue on modern architecture:

> *The formal qualities, the configuration of lines and shapes on these skins stretched over supporting structures are eloquent, very telling through their Modernist references. The grids, the pre-fab repetitions. The 'abstract' vernaculars – these all suggest a kind of certainty supposed to come with science and mathematics.*[9]

During Birmingham's Artfest in September 2007, the Friends of the Central Library mounted a film and slideshow event entitled 'Madin Birmingham' in the Library Theatre.[10] Concrete Creations, a group of young artists and curators, designed an art trail in and around the Central Library which made the visitor look at and appreciate the library building and see modernist concrete architecture through artists' eyes. So often one's eyes are on the escalator handrail, the floor, the bookcase, the video screen, and never up or around. The inclusion of the *Six Men* documentary in the Flatpack Film Festival on 15 March 2009 showed how much the younger generation had taken Madin's work to their hearts. The showing was held at the Ikon Eastside, after which the large audience stayed to listen to a short talk by Catherine O'Flynn (b.1970), the Costa-prizewinning local author.

The council applied in 2007 for a Certificate of Immunity from Listing for the library. In November 2009, the government again rejected English Heritage's recommendation that the library be listed, and approved the council's application. Those who opposed the decision immediately applied for a departmental review, which was refused by the minister in 2011.

In the catalogue of Perry Roberts's exhibition at the Ikon Gallery, the architect Owen Luder, past president of the RIBA, wrote that 'there is a growing appreciation that not all 60s buildings are as bad as the media at times portrays. A far more objective judgement has emerged based on an understanding of the potential for retention and modernising rather than the "lynch mob" mentality of those who call for their immediate demolition, too often without ensuring in advance [that the] replacement development will be better than renovating what exists.'[11]

The Central Library remains a powerful and dignified suite of buildings. The case for its renovation was well made by architect Cristina Gardiner in 2009. In concluding her Masters dissertation, she wrote: 'Free from the negative baggage that Brutalism engenders in the middle-class and middle-aged, the younger generation are extremely interested and stimulated by Brutalist architecture.' In her view, Brutalism was still 'raw but fresh' and 'as radical as the day it was created' and had to be preserved for future generations rather than ignored at everyone's peril.'[12]

Notes

1. A. Sutcliffe and R. Smith, *Birmingham 1939–1970*, 1974, p429. In the past, the city council had taken pride in the fact that Manzoni, a qualified architect, could take charge of engineering, town planning and architecture. Some council members believed (c.1950) that a separate architect's department could do layout and design work more quickly, thus speeding up the output of houses.
2. Nikolaus Pevsner and Alexandra Wedgwood, *The Buildings of England, Warwickshire*, 1966, pp115–16.
3. Professor Colin Buchanan's idea of putting pedestrians on platforms above the traffic as illustrated in *Traffic in Towns*, 1963, was very influential at the time, despite his warnings that it would not be feasible to apply it wholesale across existing cities such as London and Birmingham.
4. John Ericsson in conversation with Andy Foster, 7 October 2003. The editors are very grateful to Andy Foster for sharing his notes of this interview and for his ideas about the building.
5. Andy Foster, *Pevsner Architectural Guides: Birmingham*, 2005, p80.
6. Alan Brooks and Nikolaus Pevsner, *Worcestershire*, 2007, pp90 and 552.
7. Birmingham City Council, Annual Report 1988–9, p6.
8. 'Back to the Modern' was curated by Alan Clawley, and held in the Central Library during September 2006.
9. Jonathan Watkins Foreword in Perry Roberts, *Transition*, exhibition catalogue, 2006. Exhibition curated by Nigel Prince at the Ikon Gallery, Birmingham, 29 November 2006–21 January 2007.
10. This event included a screening of the *Six Men* film from 1965. Colour slides by Andy Foster, and the images first seen in 'Back to the Modern', 2006, were also shown.
11. Owen Luder, 'Observations on architecture and the 1960s', in Roberts, *op. cit.*
12. Cristina Gardiner, 'Birmingham Central Library: a Brutalist Building – a case study towards a constructive conservation approach', p55. Dissertation submitted by Maria Cristina Gardiner towards the Degree of Master of Science in the Conservation of Historic Buildings at the University of Bath, Department of Architecture and Civil Engineering, Session 2008–09.

Postscript

John Madin consistently produced buildings of the highest quality throughout his career. All of them deserve to be valued as worthy manifestations of 20th-century architecture and because of their inherent soundness of construction. Yet there are people who would destroy some of them without a qualm in the name of 'progress'.

It is the received wisdom that the old must make way for the new, unless it is such an important part of a community's past that it can be saved as 'heritage'. Some of Madin's 20th-century work is now seen by such admirers as English Heritage, the Twentieth Century Society and the Friends of the Central Library as deserving listed status. This has not yet been accepted by the government nor by the owners of some significant, threatened Madin buildings. While the success of the Ironbridge Gorge Museum has shown that heritage can be a marketable commodity in today's world, it is harder to show that a public library and a commercial office block could generate income for their owners by trading on the public's fascination with the past.[1] More imagination needs to be applied by the owners of such buildings when interest in their conservation begins to emerge.

Not all of Madin's buildings will be regarded as heritage in the formal sense, but there are other reasons why they should be kept for as long as possible and adapted to new uses. The steep rise in oil prices in 1974 signalled an awareness that natural resources cannot be exploited indefinitely. The rising level of carbon dioxide in the atmosphere from fossil fuel use, now understood to be a cause of climate change, can be mitigated by conserving the energy embodied in existing buildings and not using new energy to replace them. Madin anticipated the theme of the 1992 Rio Summit on Development and Environment in his own way, with his efforts to reconcile elements of the natural environment on the Calthorpe Estate or the Welsh coast with residential or commercial development.

The assumption that property prices will always rise was shattered by the collapse of the market in 2007, which has at least delayed the demolition of the Chamber of Commerce and Birmingham's NatWest tower. Meanwhile, the Federation of Engineering Employers and the Masonic Lodge appear happy with their buildings. The leaseholders of the Calthorpe Estate cannot dispose of property because of the terms of their leases and restrictive covenants. Madin's estate at Aberdyfi limits the freedom of its leaseholders to benefit personally from rising land values. In this way, Madin has done what lies within his power to protect his work from economic forces.

How can the changing public perception of the architecture of Madin's era be explained? Madin's work is not homogeneous, and different styles and periods evoke a different response. His 'Swedish style' can be seen in the Engineering Employers

opposite: Queens Square, West Bromwich, c.1975

above: Hellman's 'Birmingham Blockage' cartoon

Federation building and in the apartments, houses and tower blocks of the leafy Calthorpe Estate. The popularity of Swedish home furnishing is evidence of the extent to which Scandinavian design is liked by Britons, and it is not surprising that Madin's most humane work has on the whole remained popular and well cared for.

The *Post and Mail* building and Pebble Mill belonged to Madin's foray into the phase of modern architecture often called the 'International Style'. Birmingham people, and perhaps the English in general, have never fully embraced this style – which originated from central Europe, sometimes via the USA. Both buildings have been demolished. However, economic and technological factors were more telling than aesthetic ones in securing their demolition.

Madin's Brutalist work is exemplified by the Birmingham Central Library. This has been the butt of reactionary criticism of the 'mistakes' of the 1960s, which are held to include the sins of universal public services, the welfare state, town planning and, worst of all, exposed concrete. Did it come to symbolise an era that people wanted to forget? Buildings gestated during the 1960s came to be seen by some, including the Birmingham Civic Society, as 'socialist' and a reminder of the harsh state-sponsored architecture of Eastern Europe. Interestingly, most of the detractors of the library are business people while its supporters tend to be artists.

Madin's late phase, embracing elements of Postmodernism, comprises Metropolitan House and Neville House; it presaged the current architectural fashion for faceted or shiny surfaces, recently exemplified in Birmingham by Future Systems' Selfridges store and the proposed concourse of New Street Station. Metropolitan House and Neville House seem, for now at least, to be secure and to appeal to the people of Birmingham, accustomed as they once were to making smooth and sparkling objects such as motor cars, jewellery and toys.

Many factors beyond Madin's control have thus determined, and will continue to determine, the fate of his buildings, but the care and skill with which he designed them is beyond dispute. It is the skill with which Madin deals with a number of contradictory factors that marks his work. His efforts to reconcile development and conservation, the machine aesthetic and the Arts and Crafts tradition, human-made shelter and nature should inspire us all – not just architects and planners. His reputation will stand the test of time.

In recognition of his enormous contribution to the industrial life of his home city and region, the West Midlands Royal Institute of British Architects honoured Madin by awarding him the 2005 Service to Industry Award. The accolade was thoroughly deserved and opportune given the growing public awareness of his work, especially with the demolition of some of his best buildings and threats to others. Ian Standing summed up his citation thus:

> At a time when some of [Madin's] buildings have already gone and others are under threat, it is timely to contemplate the career of Birmingham's pre-eminent post-war architect. John was driven by a passion from his studies and architectural tours. He liked drama in his buildings, and had a strong sense for conceptual ideas, which shows in the clarity of much of the finished work: he also had the rigour to pursue these through to completion. Above all he was committed to bringing modern design to his home city. He had a highly developed business sense which gave him a unique appeal to clients and in all he was a consummate ambassador for the practice.[2]

It is hoped that this book will make a valuable and timely contribution to the promotion of public awareness of Madin's work. All the buildings outlined here deserve intelligent stewardship of the kind that is exemplified by the Engineering Employers Federation, the Wilsons of Beech Lanes, and many others.

Notes

1. Patrick Wright, in *On Living in an Old Country*, Oxford University Press, 2009 edition, p49, writes, '… the relation between capitalist property interests and the preservation of heritage sites has remained fraught throughout the [20th] century. Capitalist property relations can only be preserved if they are reproduced through new accumulative cycles, and preservation of these relations seems in this sense to necessitate the constant transformation of life in both town and country. The preservation of capital is therefore predicated on widespread social change and, indeed, actual demolition.'

2. Ian Standing, in the (unpublished) text of his speech at the RIBA in 'John Madin: RIBA West Midlands Service To Industry Award' (Citation address), 2007.

List of Works

The following list of works provides a guide to the planning and architectural commissions of John Madin FRIBA under the practice names described in this book. Owing to the extent of his work, it is a representative selection taken from the schedule of John Madin's principal commissions, which will be available in full at www.john-madin.info

The location is Birmingham unless stated otherwise.

A double asterisk (**) indicates that the building has been demolished. A single (*) indicates that it has been drastically altered, sometimes beyond recognition.

John H. D. Madin, Chartered Architect

1952–4

Building society offices **
16 Bennett's Hill
Client: Birmingham Citizens' Permanent Building Society
Architects' Journal, 9 August 1956, p216

House for Mr Page

1953–5

Private house
Grassmoor Road, King's Norton, West Midlands
Client: Mr Alan Page
House Beautiful, October 1955, pp44–8

1954–7

Shopping centre
Hillwood Road, Woodcock Hill
Client: Birmingham City Council (with City Architect)
Birmingham Mail, 4 March 1958

opposite: No.54 Hagley Road and Lyndon House, 2010

1954–5

Shoe shop
Standishgate, Wigan, Lancashire; and
28 other branches
countrywide, 1954–70
Client: Englands Shoes
Leonard Fairclough News, July 1955

1954–7

Private house
Ullenhall Lane, Redditch, West
Midlands
Client: Mr D. W. Jenkinson

1954–7

Regional HQ offices
St James's House, Frederick Road
Client: Engineering & Allied Employers
Federation
Birmingham Post & Gazette, 11 July 1957
Architect and Building News, 2 April 1958,
pp448–54
Architects' Journal, 10 April 1958, pp549–54
Architectural Review, April 1958, pp236–9
Civic Trust Award 1960 Commendation

1955–65

Carpet mill
Bloxham, near Banbury, Oxfordshire
Client: I & C Steele Ltd
Financial Times, 12 June 1965

Steeles carpet mill, Banbury, c.1960

1955–60

Regional HQ offices, banking hall and
offices to let
75 Harborne Road
Client: Birmingham Chamber of Commerce
Birmingham Post, 2 December 1960,
Supplement
Guardian, 2 December 1960
Financial Times, 9 January 1961, Architecture
To-day No. 507
Industrial Architecture, January–February 1961,
pp36–42
Builder, 28 April 1961, pp797–800
Architectural Review, April 1961, pp276–7
Interbuild, May 1961, pp31–2
RIBA Journal, March 1962, p82
RIBA Bronze Medal 1961

1956–9

Private house
10 Heaton Drive
Client: Mr E. T. Woolf
Architect and Building News, 27 January 1960,
p114

1956–9

Golf clubhouse
Monkspath, Stratford Road, Shirley,
West Midlands
Client: Shirley Golf Club
Architect and Building News, 27 January 1960,
p116

1956–8

Master plan
Edgbaston
Client: Calthorpe Estate
Manchester Guardian and *The Times*,
11 March 1958
Birmingham Mail, 14 March 1958
The Times, 21 October 1958
Birmingham Post, 1 December 1959
TV Times, 16 October 1960, p19
Ideal Home, January 1961, pp37–8
Financial Times, 12 September 1961
Financial Times, 16 November 1961,
Architecture To-day No. 522
Birmingham Post, 21 June 1962
Sphere, 20 July 1963, pp100–5
Sunday Telegraph, 10 January 1965
Birmingham Post, 20 May 1966, Supplement

1957–60

Department store and offices –
Donne House *
12 Calthorpe Road
Client: Daniel Neal
Birmingham Sketch, July 1960, pp72–3
Architect and Building News, 27 January 1961,
p138

1957–9

Apartments – Beechcroft and Fairlawn
St George's Close, Westbourne Road
Client: Artizans/Vista Developments
Limited
Birmingham Mail, 13 October 1958
Birmingham Mail, 19 October 1959
Civic Trust Award 1960 Commendation

1957–60

Private house *
15 [20] St George's Close
Client: John Madin
Financial Times, 12 September 1961
Daily Mail, 30 December 1964
Birmingham Post, 20 May 1966, Supplement
Birmingham Post, 3 July 1991

1958–62

HQ office – Shell-Mex House [HSBC]
Calthorpe Road
Client: Norwich Union
Guardian and *Financial Times*, 8 January 1960
Birmingham Post, 15 June 1962
Architects' Journal, 8 August 1962, pp349–50
Interbuild, November 1962, pp14–16

1958–64

Local centre – Western Heart, mixed
residential in 2 phases
Chad Square, Hawthorne Road
Client: Calthorpe Estates/Artizans

1958–62

Private house **
16 Oldnall Road, Kidderminster,
Worcestershire
Client: Mr Neville Tranter
Warwickshire & Worcestershire Magazine,
April 1962, pp61–3
Ideal Home & Gardening, October 1962, p45

1958–64

Housing – phase 1
Beech Lanes
Client: Artizans/Vista Developments
Limited
Birmingham Mail, 29 July 1961
Financial Times, 14 August 1962
Architectural Design, September 1962, p405
Sphere, 20 July 1963, pp100–5

1958–61

Apartments – Stonebury and Elmhurst
Norfolk Road
Client: Artizans
Architect and Building News, 25 January 1961,
p115

Stonebury and Elmhurst

Ideal Home, January 1961, pp37–8
Birmingham Mail, 29 July 1961
Architectural Review, July 1961, p55
Financial Times, 16 November 1961,
Architecture To-day No. 522

1959–62

Master plan for redevelopment –
Ladywell Centre
Hurst Street
Client: The Gooch Estate
Financial Times, *Birmingham Post*, *Guardian*
and *Daily Telegraph*, 31 August 1962

1959–64

Mixed residential in 3 phases
Pinewoods Avenue, West Hagley,
West Midlands
Client: J. Harper & Sons

1959–61

Apartments and 12-storey block –
Elmwood Court
Pershore Road
Client: Property & General Investment
Birmingham Mail, 23 September 1960
Birmingham Post, 28 October 1961

1959–62

HQ offices – Arthur Thompson House
[CIBA]
146–50 Hagley Road
Client: West Midlands Regional Hospital
Board/Artizans
Sphere, 20 July 1963, pp100–5

1959–62

**Bank, offices and shops – College
House ****
Aston Street
Client: Holloway Developments/Lloyds
Bank

College House, c.1964

1959–62

**Apartments and 13-storey block –
Chadbrook Crest**
**Harborne Road/Brook Road/Richmond
Hill Road**
Client: Artizans/Vista Developments
Limited
Birmingham Mail, 29 July 1961

1959–62

Bank and offices – Radclyffe House
66–8 Hagley Road
Clients: Bernard Sunley Investment Trust/
Martins Bank
(John Madin & Partners offices, 1963–7)

1959–66

**Offices and retail – Broadgate House/
Rail House [Quayside Tower]**
Broad Street
Client: Holloway Developments
Building, 13 June 1969, pp93–100

1959–61

**Apartments and 14-storey block –
West Point**
Westfield Road/Hermitage Road
Client: Artizans/Vista Developments
Limited
Birmingham Mail, 18 November 1961

1959–61

**Apartments and 12-storey block –
High Point**
Richmond Hill Road
Client: Holloway Developments
Birmingham Post, 20 June 1962
Architects' Journal, 19 September 1962, p128
Sphere, 20 July 1963, pp100–5

1959–66

Newspaper printing works and offices *
Colmore Circus
Client: *Birmingham Post & Mail*
Financial Times, 9 December 1964
Architects' Journal, 8 December 1965,
pp1385–1406
Interior Design, January 1966, pp8–14
Architect and Building News, 27 April 1966,
pp31–2
Building, 3 June 1966, pp68–71
Architects' Journal, 18 April 1973, pp911–24
* Printing works remain

1960–2

**Master plan for new seaside holiday
village – Bron-y-Mor
Tywyn, Gwynedd, Wales**
Client: Bishton Holdings
Liverpool Post, 7 July 1961
Daily Express, 25 and 26 July 1961
Architects' Journal, 25 July 1961, p110
Official Architecture & Planning, August 1961,
pp365–6
Liverpool Post, 26 September 1962
Ideal Home, July 1963, pp37–8
Western Mail, 11 September 1964

1960–1

**Mixed residential
Westbourne Gardens**
Client: W. Scrase
Warwickshire & Worcestershire Magazine,
September 1961, pp38–41

1960–2

**Housing – Cala Drive/Estria Road/
Carpenters Road/Wheeleys Road**
Client: Artizans/Vista Developments
Limited
Sphere, 20 July 1963, pp100–5
Ministry of Housing and Local Government
Award 1964

1960–2

**Apartments, 16-storey block –
Warwick Crest
Carpenter's Road/Arthur Road**
Client: Artizans/Vista Developments Ltd

1960–6

**UK HQ offices, 15-storey block
Banner Lane, Coventry, West Midlands**
Client: Massey Ferguson

1960–3

**Apartments and 12–storey block
– Woodbourne
Augustus Road/Norfolk Road**
Client: Artizans/Vista Developments Ltd

1960–3

**16-storey office building – Lyndon
House
58–62 Hagley Road**
Client: Bernard Sunley Investment Trust
Architects' Journal, January 1962
Sphere, 20 July 1963, pp100–5
Building, 13 June 1969, pp93–100

1961–71

**Regional television and radio centre ★★
Pebble Mill Lane**
Client: British Broadcasting Corporation
The Times, 13 November 1962
Architectural Design, December 1962, p556
Financial Times, 10 November 1971
Birmingham Post, 11 November 1971,
Supplement
Building, 11 February 1972, pp53–60
Technique des Travaux, January/February 1973,
pp17–26

Warwick Crest, c.1963

1961-3

Seaside holiday village, phases 1 and 2 – Bron-y-Mor
Tywyn, Gwynedd, Wales
Client: Bishton Holdings
Liverpool Post, 26 September 1962
Ideal Home Magazine, July 1963, pp46–7
Western Mail, Express & Star, 11 September 1964
Ministry of Housing and Local Government Award 1964

1961-5

16-storey office building – Hagley House [Cobalt Square]
Hagley Road
Client: Bernard Sunley Investment Trust
Building, 13 June 1969, pp93–100

Hagley House, c.1966

1961-4

6-storey office block, canteen and alterations to existing buildings in 3 phases – Hawthorns House
Halfords Lane, Smethwick, West Midlands
Client: Henry Hope & Sons
Financial Times, 22 September 1964
Architects' Journal, 2 December 1964, pp1319–21

1961-6

5-storey office block, first of three buildings of the same design, client and site, Beaufort House (1969–75), Duchess House 1973–75
123 Hagley Road
Client: Norwich Union
Birmingham Post, 27 April 1967
Building Design, 29 September 1972
Civic Trust Award 1969
(John Madin Design Group offices, 1967 onwards)

1961-7

Regional HQ, 8-storey administration block
Haslucks Green Road, Solihull, West Midlands
Client: Central Electricity Generating Board
Civic Trust Award 1969

1961–6

Halls of residence
82 Farquhar Road
Client: Queens Ecumenical Theological
College
Birmingham Post, 23 May 1964
Building, 19 January 1973, pp56–8
Architects' Journal, 6 June 1976, pp1083–95

Queens College

1962–5

Apartments – Wake Green Park
Belle Walk
Client: Sir Alfred McAlpine

1962–5

Two terraces of 4-bedroom houses
Clare Drive and Grenfell Drive
Client: W. Scrase

1962–3

Master plan, hotel, shopping and social
centre, apartments
L'Erée, Guernsey
Client: Mrs Southall

1962–5

New town extension and town-centre
master plan
Client: Corby Development Corporation/
Ministry of Housing and Local Government
Corby Evening Telegraph, 23 July 1964
Birmingham Post, 29 July 1964
Financial Times, 30 July 1964
Corby Leader, 7 August 1964

John H. D. Madin & Partners

1962–7

New hall of residence – Lucas House
[Pritchatts House]
9 Pritchatts Road
Client: University of Birmingham

Lucas House (Pritchatts House)

1962–5

Master plan for town centre: phased
redevelopment
West Bromwich, West Midlands
Client: West Bromwich Corporation (with
Borough Engineer)
Birmingham Post, 27 July 1962
Builder, 13 December 1963, pp1215–16
Official Architecture & Planner, January 1964,
pp61 and 63
Financial Times and *The Times*, 9 February 1965
Architect & Building News, 10 February 1965, p259

1962–4

Worcester Expansion Study
Client: Ministry of Housing and Local
Government
Birmingham Post, 6 November 1962
Financial Times, 7 November 1962
Architectural Design, December 1962, p555
Birmingham Post, 10 March 1963
Guardian, 10 March 1964

1963–9

**Theatre foyer extension and shops –
Alexandra Theatre
Suffolk Street Queensway**
Client: Alexandra Theatre/Ringway
Properties (N)

1963–6

**Conversion of house to provide lecture,
tutorial and common rooms, warden
quarters, new library – Winterbourne
Edgbaston Park Road**
Client: University of Birmingham

1963–6

**Apartment block – Balholm
Mucklow Hill, Halesowen, West
Midlands**
Client: J. Harper & Sons

1963–7

**Housing contracts 1 and 2 – 450
dwellings – Brookside
Gainsborough Road, Kingswood,
Corby, Northamptonshire**
Client: Corby Development Corporation

1963–7

**Plan for Dawley New Town
Dawley, Shropshire**
Client: Dawley Development Corporation/
Ministry for Housing and Local
Government
Financial Times and *Guardian*, 20 January 1965
Surveyor & Municipal Engineer, 23 January 1965,
pp17, 33–4 and 37–8
Architects' Journal, 27 January 1965, pp214 and
221–4

1963–8

**Church
Littleton Street, West Bromwich,
West Midlands**
Client: Church of the Good Shepherd with
St John

1964–71

**Masonic temple, lodge rooms,
ballroom, dining and entertainment
facilities [Clarendon Suites see
image p.iv]
Clarendon Road/Hagley Road**
Client: Warwickshire Masonic Temple
Properties Ltd
Architects' Journal, 5 March 1972, pp497–510
Brick Bulletin, March 1972, pp11–15
Interior Design, December 1972, p831

1964–7

**Apartments
Maney Hill/St Peters Close/Birmingham
Road, Sutton Coldfield, West Midlands**
Client: Second Bromford Housing Society

1964–75

Bank and offices. Phase 1: banking hall and ancillary offices, offices to let in blocks of 5 and 9 storeys; phase 2: 16-storey tower and 20-storey tower
Colmore Row
Client: National Westminster Bank
Building, 10 October 1975, p63
Birmingham Post, October 1975
Financial Times, 5 July 1976

1964–71

Newspaper works and offices
Wellington Street, Leeds
Client: *Yorkshire Post*
Architects' Journal, 4 August 1971, pp226–7
Building, 12 November 1971, pp111–18
RIBA Regional Award 1971

1964–5

Civic-centre master plan
Client: Birmingham City Corporation
(with City Architect)
Birmingham Evening Mail & Despatch, 25 May 1965
Financial Times, *Guardian* and *The Times*, 26 May 1965

1964–73

Central Library, bus interchange and Chamberlain Square
Paradise Circus
Client: Birmingham City Council
(with City Architect)
Birmingham Post, 23 September 1967
Birmingham Post, 2 August 1968
Financial Times, 23 July 1973
Birmingham Post, 22 November 1973
Building, 7 December 1973, pp87–94
Municipal Journal, 1 February 1974

Building, 8 February 1974, pp36–7
Architects' Journal, 22 May 1974, pp1138–56
Interior Design, May 1974, pp292–5
Birmingham Post, 8 January 1976

1964–73

School of Music, recital room, teaching studios, practice studios
Paradise Circus
Client: Birmingham City Council
(with City Architect)

1965–72

Master layout and design of high-density housing – Calthorpe Park CDA
Pershore Road
Client: Birmingham City Council
(with City Architect)

1965–6

Lecture Theatre
Cuddesdon, Oxfordshire
Client: Ripon Theological College

1965–71

Town-centre redevelopment – Phase one, Queen's Square: 60 shops, 2 supermarkets, bus station and multi-storey car park
West Bromwich, West Midlands
Client: West Bromwich Corporation
Architectural Design, May 1972, p281
Architectural Review, March 1973, p176

1965–9

Plan for Telford New Town
Telford, Shropshire
Client: Ministry of Housing and Local

Government and Telford Development Corporation
Birmingham Post, 17 July 1969
Town & Country Planning, September 1969, pp416–19
Building, 18 June 1976, pp79–82

1966–7

Master layout and design, private seaside residential development of 12 hectares (30 acres)
Church Street/Balkan Hill, Aberdyfi, Gwynedd, Wales
Client: John Madin

1967–77

Phased housing development – co-ownership apartments and warden-controlled flats
[Wake Green Park]

1967–70, 1971–2, 1971–4, 1974–7

Belle Walk
Client: Bromford Housing Association
Housing Review, January/February 1976, pp15–16

1967–75

Self-catering holiday village, including Eastwards – Aberdovey Hillside Park
Aberdyfi, Gwynedd, Wales
Client: John Madin

John Madin Design Group

1967–9

Tennis clubhouse
Sugarloaf Lane, Stourbridge, West Midlands
Client: Stourbridge Lawn Tennis Club

1967–72

Divisional police headquarters, offices, stables and garage
New Street, West Bromwich, West Midlands
Client: West Midlands Police Authority

Police headquarters, West Bromwich

1968–78

Offices: two towers, 18 and 9 storeys
44–56 Hagley Road [54 Hagley Road]
Client: Commercial Union/Neville Industrial Securities

1968–77

Offices and retail – Metropolitan House [No.1 Hagley Road], 18-storey tower on parking podium, offices and supermarket, and the Broadway building Five Ways
Client: MEPC
Birmingham Post, 26 April 1973

1968–75

Master housing layout and detailed design of 730 dwellings – Brookside Stirchley, Telford
Client: Telford Development Corporation

1969–75

15-storey offices – Coventry Point Hertford Precinct, Coventry, West Midlands
Client: Bryant Samuel
Surveyor, 27 February 1976, p6
Building Design, 27 February 1976, p7
Building Specification, October 1976, pp41–2
Architecture West Midlands, December 1976, pp43–4
Arup Journal, December 1978, pp10–18

1970–5

Town-centre redevelopment – Phase two, King's Square: 36 shops, department store and market hall West Bromwich, West Midlands
Client: West Bromwich Corporation
Estate Times, 28 March 1974
Estate Gazette, 30 March 1974
Financial Times, 13 September 1974
Municipal Journal, 26 September 1975

1970–4

Public houses
Client: Mitchells & Butlers
The Farriers, West Bromwich, West Midlands
Interior Design, February 1973, pp104–5
The Florin, Brookfield Precinct
Building, 4 October 1974, pp80–2
Interior Design, February 1975, p104
The Centurion, Chester Road; The Merrymaker, Daren Close; The Friendly Inn, Gloucester Way
Brick Bulletin, March 1973, pp17–24

1970

Plan for a new village
Grafton Flyford, Worcester, Worcestershire
Client: The Graves Organisation Ltd
Architects' Journal, 17 May 1972, pp1074–5

1970–5

Offices behind retained façade of Grade II listed Georgian terrace – Regency House
97–107 Hagley Road
Client: Rentcroft Investments Limited
Estate Gazette, 22 January 1976, p212

1971–6

Central Library
Redditch, West Midlands
Client: Redditch Urban District Council
The Times, 16 March 1976
Redditch Indicator, 17 September 1976

1971–4

Regional headquarters **
Fanum House, Dog Kennel Lane,
Halesowen, West Midlands
Client: Automobile Association
Financial Times, 30 January 1974
Brick Bulletin, May 1974, pp8–11
Architects' Journal, 11 December 1974,
pp1371–82

1971–7

Apartments in two phases – Jacoby
Close
Priory Road
Client: Braxel Properties Ltd/David Charles
Ltd

1972–5

Offices – Belmont House
40 Vicarage Road/Ivy Bush
Client: Calthorpe Estate
Glass Age, February 1976, pp26–7

Belmont House

1972–4

Grosvenor Shopping Centre, Phase 2
Northfield
Client: Grosvenor Estates
Evening Mail, 24 January 1973
Birmingham Post, 25 January 1973

1972–6

Banking hall and offices – Neville
House
Harborne Road
Client: G. R. Dawes Ltd – Neville Industrial
Securities
Architects' Journal, 16 April 1977, pp620–2
RIBA Journal, August 1977
RIBA Regional Award 1979

1973–5

Plans for marinas, associated facilities,
housing
Port Hamble, Southampton; and at
Hythe, Exmouth and Swansea
Client: Rank Marine International

1973–5

Redevelopment plan – Worcester Bar
Gas Street Basin
Client: British Waterways/Copthall
Holdings Ltd

1974–6

Apartments – St Anne's Court
Park Hill
Client: Second Bromford Housing
Association

1974–8

Sheltered housing – The Oaks
Berryfield Road, Sutton Coldfield, West
Midlands
Client: Anchor Housing Association

1974–81

Mixed residential, including sheltered
housing, 400 dwellings and local shops
on 11 hectares (27 acres) – Tanyard
Farm
Tanners Lane/Banner Lane, Coventry,
West Midlands
Client: The Housing Corporation

**John Madin Design Group
International**

1966–72

Hilltop holiday village, first phase –
Wardija Hill Top Village
St Paul's Bay, Malta
Client: A consortium

1968–9

Plan for the development of 5
kilometres (3 miles) of Tripoli's
coastline
Mellaha Highway, Tripoli, Libya
Client: Libyan Ministry of Tourism

1968–74

Mixed residential and tourist development of 80 houses and apartments
with club and shops – Peace Hill
Kyrenia, Cyprus
Client: Renos Solomides

1968–74

Plan for new town on 400 hectares
(1,000 acres): 6,000 dwellings, hotels,
shopping, golf courses
Lara, western Cyprus
Client: Renos Solomides

1970–5

Combined radio and television centre
Slavonska Avenija, Zagreb, Croatia
Client: The Marconi Company for
Yugoslavian Radio Television

1973–5

Design proposals for 1,000-berth
marina and 800 residential units
Port d'Hyères, France
Client: Rank Marine International

1980–9

Master plan for 100 hectares (240
acres): 300 houses and apartments
within a golf course and a business
park, with offices up to 8 storeys in
landscaped setting – Mays Landing
Hamilton Township, New Jersey, USA
Client: Lordland Inc.

John Madin FRIBA

1975–present

Self-catering holiday village: additional
dwellings and facilities – Aberdovey
Hillside Village
Aberdyfi, Gwynedd, Wales
Client: Hillside Parks Ltd

1992–present

Houses and apartments in landscaped
setting – Aberdovey Hillside Park
Aberdyfi, Gwynedd, Wales
Client: Hillside Parks Ltd

1996–8

Yacht clubhouse
Hamble, near Southampton, Hampshire
Client: Royal Southern Yacht Club

Bibliography

Birmingham City Council, *Edgbaston Conservation Area No. 15*. 1:12,000-scale map produced in 1975, showing the designated Conservation Area.

Birmingham City Council Planning Department, *70s Birmingham Buildings*, Birmingham City Council, 1997.

Alan Brooks and Nikolaus Pevsner, *The Buildings of England, Worcestershire*, London, Yale University Press, 2007.

Calthorpe Estate, *An Introduction to the Calthorpe Estate Redevelopment Proposals*, Birmingham, Calthorpe Estate, 1958.

David Chapman (ed.), *Region and Renaissance 1950 to 2000*, Royal Town Planning Institute (West Midlands Branch), 2000.

Maurice de Soissons, *Telford, the Making of Shropshire's New Town*, Telford, Sarah Hill Press, 1991.

Andy Foster, *Pevsner Architectural Guides: Birmingham*, London, Yale University Press, 2005.

Olga Franklin, 'This is the house Britain's busiest architect built for himself ...', *Daily Mail*, 30 December 1964.

Cristina Gardiner, 'Birmingham Central Library: a Brutalist Building – a case study towards a constructive conservation approach' (M.Sc. Conservation of Historic Buildings dissertation, University of Bath, 2009).

Lynsey Hanley, *Estates – an intimate history*, London, Granta, 2007.

Richard Haslam, Julian Orbach and Adam Voelcker, *The Buildings of Wales, Gwynedd*, London, Yale University Press, 2009.

Douglas Hickman, *Birmingham*, London, Studio Vista, 1970.

John Madin Design Group, *Telford Development Proposals*, Volume 1, Birmingham, John Madin Design Group, 1969.

Ian Latham and Mark Swenarton (eds.), *Brindleyplace*, London, Right Angle Publishing, 1999.

John Madin, 'Design and Development of Marinas and Environmental Considerations', unpublished paper, c.1994.

Hilary Millward, *Window on Edgbaston*, Birmingham, Calthorpe Estate, 1962.

John Newman and Nikolaus Pevsner, *The Buildings of England, Shropshire*, London, Yale University Press, 2006.

Juhani Pallasmaa, *The Thinking Hand – Existential and Embodied Wisdom in Architecture*, Chichester, Wiley, 2009.

Nikolaus Pevsner, *An Outline of European Architecture*, Harmondsworth, Pelican, 1942.

Nikolaus Pevsner, *The Buildings of England, Shropshire*, Harmondsworth, Penguin Books, 1966.

opposite: **Aberdovey Hillside Park and Village**

Nikolaus Pevsner and Alexandra
    Wedgwood, *The Buildings of England,
    Warwickshire*, Harmondsworth,
    Penguin Books, 1966.
Perry Roberts, *Transition* [exhibition
    catalogue], Birmingham, Ikon Gallery,
    2006.
Philip Smith, 'Architect joins house fight.
    Extension "would ruin prototype"',
    Birmingham Post, 20 June 1990.

Anthony Sutcliffe and Roger Smith,
    Birmingham 1939–1970, London,
    Oxford University Press, 1974.
Patrick Wright, *On Living in an Old
    Country*, Oxford, Oxford University
    Press, 2009 edition.

John Madin practices up to 1975

John H. D. Madin Chartered Architect 1950 to 1962

Sole Principal: John Madin

John H. D. Madin & Partners 1962 to 1967

Senior Partner: John Madin
Junior Partners: Tom Hood, Douglas Smith, Clifford Downing

The John Madin Design Group 1967 to 1975

Senior Partner: John Madin
Junior Partners: Derek E Davis, Michael Heywood, Michael E Holt
Salaried Partners: J E H Taylor, J N Ericsson, D K Graham-Cumming, L T Jones,
F Mark, R K Wood, M J Smith
Associates: A D V Hickman, J Mansell
Group Secretary: R Harrison
Secretary to John Madin: Kay Collings
Librarian. Research & Information: E Grizzell

JMDG GROUP PHOTOGRAPH
The people in the group photograph taken outside 123 Hagley Road around 1976 are
(p 17), to the best of Frank Brophy's knowledge; Mike Holt, Mike Heywood, John Madin,
Derek Davis, Kay Colling, Lewis Jones, John Ericsson, Jim Hook, Eric Grimwood, John
Knight, Beryl Thomas, Ray Wood, Ted Grizzell, Mike Clarke, Tom Wright, Pamela
Brown, John Mansell, John Wood, Walley Maher, Brian Rose, Cyril Cox, Harry Taylor,
John Davies, Douglas Hickman, Garry Donby, Duncan Bainbridge, Duncan Sharp.

Index

Picture Credits

The author and publisher have made every effort to contact copyright holders and will be happy to correct, in subsequent editions, any errors or omissions that are brought to their attention.

Archive photographs by known photographers:
John Madin collection – Henk Snoek – front cover, p38, John Whybrow – x, Birmingham Post – 4, 10 (top), 129, Logan Photography – 9 (top), 25, 26, 27 (top), 33, 41, 55, 57, 59, 60, 66 (bottom), 70, 84, 138 (top), John Bird/ BBC – 15, 92 (top), 92 (bottom), Reilly & Constantine – 27 (middle), 29 (top), 130, Wolloughby Gullachson/BBC – 44 (top), 44 (bottom), 45, Aleksander Karolyi – 72. Frank Brophy collection – F Jewell-Harrison – 79 (bottom)

Archive photographs by unknown photographers:
John Madin collection – 9 (bottom), xii, 13 (top), 20, 23 (top) (Calthorpe Estates), 27 (middle), 28, 31 (top), 31 (bottom), 34, 35 (top), 35 (bottom right), 37 (top), 40, 42, 47, 51, 53 (top left), 53 (bottom right), 56 (bottom), 61 (right), 63, 65, 71, 77, 88 (top), 95 (top), 95 (bottom), 96 (top), 100, 102, 104, 107, 111 (top), 112, 120, 125, 126, 128, 131, 132 (left), 132 (right), 135, 137
Frank Brophy collection – 17, 58, 87, 92 (bottom)
RIBA collection – 53 (bottom left)
Barrie Hall collection – 23 (bottom)

Line drawings
John Madin collection – 6, 7, 8, 18, 22 (Calthorpe Estates), 23 (top) (Calthorpe Estates), 54, 64 (top), 67, 74, 79, 81, 83 (bottom), 86, 88 (bottom), 93, 96 (bottom), 105, 106, 108, 110

Frank Brophy collection – 77 (top), 78
Alan Clawley – 24

Artists impressions
John Madin collection – 97, 113,
Barrie Hall collection – 115
Birmingham City Council – 117 (first published in its Annual Report)

New colour photographs:
James Davies – back cover, ii, 13 (bottom left), 13 (bottom right), 18 (right), 27 (bottom), 29 (bottom), 30 (top), 30 (bottom), 32 (left), 32 (right), 35 (bottom left), 37 (bottom), 39, 43, 46, 53 (top right), 56 (top), 60 (right), 66 (top), 69, 111 (bottom).
John Madin collection – vi, 10 (bottom), 12, 35 (top), 50, 61 (top left), 61 (bottom right), 64 (bottom), 68, 90, 98 (top), 98 (bottom), 124, 140 (top), 140 (bottom).

Miscellaneous
The illustration of the Iron Bridge on the front cover of the Telford Report on p83 (top) was owned by Allied Ironfounders. Louis Hellman kindly gave his permission to include the cartoon on p122 that was first published in the Architects Journal 14 August 2008.
Ian Cuthbert designed the flier on p5 using an archive photograph from the Birmingham Central Library collection and a photograph of the exposed concrete of Madin's library taken by the author.